Tales out of school

Consumers' views of British education

Roger White
with
David Brockington

Routledge & Kegan Paul
London, Boston, Melbourne and Henley

First published in 1983
by Routledge & Kegan Paul Plc
39 Store Street, London WC1E 7DD,
9 Park Street, Boston, Mass. 02108, USA,
296 Beaconsfield Parade, Middle Park,
Melbourne, 3206, Australia, and
Broadway House, Newtown Road,
Henley-on-Thames, Oxon RG9 1EN
Set in IBM Press Roman
and printed in Great Britain by
The Thetford Press Ltd., Thetford, Norfolk
© Roger White 1983

Library of Congress Cataloging in Publication Data

White, Roger, 1948-

Tales out of school.
(Routledge education books)
1. Education – Great Britain – Case studies. 2. Education –
Great Britain – Aims and objectives. I. Brockington, David.
II. Title. III. Series.
LA210.W46 1983   370'.973   82-16644

ISBN 0-7100-9446-9

Tales out of school

Routledge Education Books

Advisory editor: John Eggleston
Professor of Education
University of Keele

Contents

v

Contents

Acknowledgments

The tradition in the world of print is to assign authorship to the individuals whose names appear on the jacket of a book, but this recognises
only one aspect of the creative process of its production, and anyway, as
with this book, the work is often unevenly split. Without the energies of
Paul Edgar and Chandra Hernandez, who transcribed most of the seventy-
seven tape recordings, the interviews would still be concealed on
chromium dioxide patterns; and without the typing skill of Jill Chapman
and Maureen Barton, the transcribed interviews would never have reached
this printed form. My two-fingered, thirty-words-a-minute effort would
have taken me until the next winter frost — by which time the promised
land of full employment and perfect schooling, predicted by politicians,
will surely have arrived! To Zeta Eastes I am indebted for the careful
hours spent in proof reading the final manuscript, and I hope her
garden hasn't suffered in consequence.

Without the support of the Joseph Rowntree Charitable Trust I
could never have afforded the travel and subsistence costs incurred
during the nine months of unpaid leave I took from my job to research and write this book with Dave Brockington. I am very grateful
for their further assistance and that of the Gane Trust in Bristol, which
covered the costs of transcribing and typing the many drafts of the
manuscript. This book owes as much to their patronage as to the
creative skill of all involved.

To Mary Tasker of Bath University and Richard Pring of Exeter
University I am very appreciative of their willingness to supervise
me during this period of research — a necessary condition for my
being granted unpaid leave. To my own employers — in particular
Tim Prime — I am thankful for the opportunity offered by this time
away from my job at the Bayswater Centre and the ROSLA Project.
I am well aware that some employers view such requests for 'unpaid
leave' with a faint aura of moral disapproval, or insist on a commitment

to a course of professional improvement on secondment, instead of just accepting that personal enrichment is as valuable a purpose. Time out doesn't necessarily lead towards a mire of mental and physical disintegration, and is as likely to offer opportunities for self-development as the safely cloistered structure of a higher degree course. I would hope that my own experience and the example of the re-conditioned model I shall bring back to my job might encourage other employers to support requests for unpaid leave — a development which seems so obviously sensible at a time of enforced unemployment for over three million people.

To David Godwin, Stratford Caldecott and Sally Gough at RKP, who have patiently answered letters and helped refine ideas and the final form of this book, I owe more than just a jar of coffee. To Ben Morris and Tom Hazlewood, whose help with *Absent with Cause* I didn't acknowledge, I hope this will redress the omission. To all those who arranged the inter-views for me in various parts of the country I am particularly indebted, because without their own involvements I could never have made contact with the seventy young people whose views are represented here. So, to Hilary Workman and Jackie Rowe in Cornwall, to Margo Gunn and Alastair Moir in Bristol, to Maggie Jager in Birmingham, to Michael Willson in Derbyshire, to Jeff Crow and Mike Allpress in Maldon, to Paul Springford in Peterborough, to Josie Dunn and Geoff Woodhead in Lancaster, to Tim Pickles and Tom Heron in Wallsend, to John Heptingstall in Whitley Bay, to Jo Richmond and helpers at the Big Lamp youth project in Newcastle, to Jim Rooney and Peter Wedell of Lothian Association of Youth Clubs, Audrey Milan of SAYC and Elizabeth Gray in Edinburgh — and to all my friends nearer at home who have encouraged me in this project, particularly Rog and Chris and Janie and Keith, who have kept the boat afloat in my 'absence' — I would just like to say thank you.

Abbreviations

CBI	Confederation of British Industry
CSE	Certificate of Secondary Education
CSV	Community Service Volunteer
CYP	Community Youth Project
DES	Department of Education and Science
GCE	General Certificate of Education
LEA	Local Education Authority
MSC	Manpower Services Commission
PBWE	Project Based Work Experience
TES	*Times Educational Supplement*
TOPS	Training Opportunities Programmes
TUC	Trades Union Congress
WEEP	Work Experience on Employers Premises
WEP	Work Experience Programme
YOP	Youth Opportunities Programme

Part one

Young people's comments
on education and leaving school to
look for work

Introduction

There is a story told about a husband and wife leading their prized donkey to market along a dusty road near Athens some time before the birth of Christ.

Ridiculed by other travellers for walking beside the animal and wasting its strength, the old man persuades his young wife to mount the beast while he leads it by the halter.

Other passers by, some of whom are aligned to the Women's Lib Movement, criticise the wife for taking it easy while her husband trudges wearily on foot. They swap places, which causes the more chivalrous male chauvinists that they meet to chide the husband for subjecting hardship on such a pretty woman.

In desperation they both mount the poor donkey, which draws cries of brutality from animal lovers, who threaten to refer them both to the ancient Greek equivalent of the RSPCA.

The only remaining alternative – that they carry the animal between them – offers endings appropriate to your sense of humour. Whether they stumble and drop it in the river Nine (giving rise to the adjective asinine to describe such behaviour), whether the old man suffers a fatal coronary, or whether the wife elopes with the first Greek equivalent of Sir Launcelot who comes along, is all really irrelevant.

The simple message – that you can't please all of the people all of the time – comes across.

And so it is with schools. As passers by, or passers through, we all have experiences and opinions that create our very individual perceptions of the institution and the value of the processes within it.

It is easy to be critical, since we can be fairly confident that no one system can ever be right for all the children required to attend it. Consequently, there will always be advocates for change. One response to such pressure would be to dismiss the voices of criticism as unrepresentative, unrealistic and irrelevant. The opposite response would be to

3

undertake sweeping reforms that then generate equally vociferous declamations from other quarters. You can please only some of the people some of the time. The struggle is always to make that 'some' as large a proportion as is possible. We are nowhere near that target.

Perhaps in looking at schools and listening to criticism of education we can avoid the rigidities embraced by extremes and ask ourselves whether, within the existing provision of resources, there are ways of improving the system so as to increase the number of young people appropriately catered for.

It is in this light that this book should be read.

It represents the experiences and perspectives of seventy young people, almost all of whom left school at sixteen, and who are now in work, or who are unemployed — or who are in the twilight world of semi-employment on the Youth Opportunities Programme.

They have been encouraged to reflect on their eleven years of compulsory schooling and offer positive comment and criticism about the processes, content and structure of the school institution, and of the world beyond its walls when they left to look for work. Their comments were recorded, transcribed and edited to produce this book.

Their remarks were often as concerned with the relationship between school and home as with the nature of the formal educational system itself and, by balancing anecdote with analysis, I have tried to present a realistic picture of what it is like to leave school at sixteen. For some of the seventy young people interviewed here during 1981, leaving school meant going straight on to the dole; for others it meant a year on YOP; for a few it meant 'real' work. The personal accounts of what it was actually like reveal the human experiences behind the official statistics about employment prospects of school leavers.

In one sense of course, the impressions of seventy people can reflect as much about the individuals they are as the systems they are examining. Their observations are bound to be tempered by the perceptual filterings of their own memories. (Do we best remember the good things or the bad moments of the past? the more immediate events or the distant happenings?) Sometimes, also, as all of us know, the criticisms we make of institutions and of others act as a way of rationalising our own personal failure.

But it would be sad if that were the only response to the words and feelings and experiences of the young people recorded here.

Of course their comments reflect individual experiences, but these experiences of success and failure are common to thousands of other young people and are very much influenced by the institutions that they, like all the others, have been through. It is only if we are absolutely convinced of the correctness of all our own policies and practices

4

in school that we could afford to dismiss their observations as minority meanderings.

In a few cases their comments highlight the inadequacies of home situations. In that sense this book illustrates further examples of class and cultural alienation from schools. But the child whose learning ability is moderated by home circumstances will have perceptions of school which are exactly those we should be sensitive to. There is sufficient empirical evidence about how social differences in this country affect school achievement of children and how factors like cramped housing, 'broken' homes and poor income apply to a large enough minority of children to warrant some policy change.

It is also true that in other cases their comments reflect the support of families who wanted them to make the most of their schooling and who, in some cases, had aspirations of university scholarships for their children. Taking the group as a whole, rarely was their leaving at sixteen an indicator of personal inadequacy, even in terms of the strictly limited way we currently measure capability in our education system.

Having distanced themselves from the institution, their perceptions of school, their reasons for leaving and their subsequent experiences of work and unemployment are certainly shared by many other young people. Though not 'representative' in a strict statistical sense, these seventy do speak for thousands of others. To satisfy the criteria of a rigorous sociological survey and obtain a 'representative' sample would have been very difficult in the given context. It would have meant selecting a random sample from each area of the country, from urban and rural districts, from middle and working class, from the affluent and the deprived, from high-rise flats and low-density housing estates, from the academically successful and the illiterate, from male and female, from manual and white-collar, from black and white, from comprehensive and selective schools. In all, it would have meant doing thousands of interviews. Since each interview represents at least ten to fifteen hours of work in terms of setting up, recording, transcribing, typing and editing, a thousand would have priced the book beyond the reach of all except those with Paul Getty-style affluence.

Instead, I have interviewed seventy young people between the ages of sixteen and twenty-three and can simply say that each of the above categorisations can be attached to at least one — and probably several — individuals within the 'sample'. On a geographic basis they range from rural Cornwall and Derbyshire to the towns of Lancaster and Peterborough; from the suburbs of Birmingham to the streets of Elswick in Newcastle; from Great Barr to Whitley Bay; from the prestigious cities of Edinburgh and Bristol to the centres of rural communities in Bodmin and Maldon.

The interviewees were selected with the help of friends in each area mentioned — people who knew young people with points of view about school and work that would be more than just anarchic and aimless. I met them in youth clubs, in training workshops, at their places of work, in their homes, in schools, in community centres and in the open air. In all cases they had been forewarned of my visit and had volunteered themselves to be interviewed.

I explained to each one that I was interested in *their* perceptions of school and work and how I felt that, although theirs was a voice rarely heard in any discussion about education, they must have comments to make about subjects, about teachers, about preparation for jobs and about possible changes that would be relevant to such discussions. I told them I wanted their honest opinions, not simply those they thought I might like to hear, and that if they were going to be critical I would push them to justify their criticisms. I promised them that their comments would be put together with those of other young people into a book that might be looked at by adults responsible for running the institutions about which they were offering comments. It was an opportunity for them to say what they really thought to the people who could actively respond if they chose to.

I had a check list of prepared questions and for an hour or so I talked with each of them individually (the exception being one group discussion in Newcastle). It was easier alone. They talked more freely and probably gave more honest answers, having no audience to play to nor friends to ridicule and remind them of their comments subsequently.

The transcribed recordings were returned to them in due course for editing, should they wish to alter or add anything. Some of them did, like the girl who asked me to score out, 'my boy friend's a right layabout and spends his dole money at the betting shop', because she'd changed boy friends. Or like the boy who typed out a complete week's timetable, incorporating his suggestions for a revised curriculum (allowing an hour a day for 'problem-solving groups'). The girl who said 'I'm amazed you managed to make any sense of it; I wish I'd been more articulate' was echoed somewhat poignantly by the boy who wrote back, 'I did not feel, honestly, that anybody takes any notice of my views. Thank you for showing me you are interested.' Only two asked for pseudonyms, and for one of them – 'Tory Crimes' – we are indebted to the punk tradition.

From the returned transcripts, which averaged twelve pages of typed comments for each person, I have had to be selective in choosing what appears in these pages. In this process many important and interesting observations have been omitted, and these unused remarks could fill several more books. But within the limitations of space for this one book I have tried to represent their opinions and ideas as fully as possible.

Some were bothered that their transcripts, with unedited grammar, made them sound 'common', so I have amended them as requested but this raises a question about how far to go in correcting grammar and risk losing the essential spontaneity of recorded comments. Their verbal expression of opinion and experience is the crucial ingredient that gives the whole book its freshness and flavour, which would have been difficult to achieve if I'd asked them to *write* their comments. For those with problems of literacy such a request would have been impossible to handle with any degree of self-fulfilment, and, for these people in particular, it was only through talking that they could convey the depth of insight and perception reproduced in these pages.

Inevitably, in transferring their words to paper, something more than just the musical fluctuations of local dialect is lost. Expressions of hope and anger, of exhilaration and despair, are difficult to reproduce in print and the nuances of innuendo and confidence become less discernible in the formality of typescript. The excitement in one lad's eyes as he described the first time on the back of a horse, the gestures of the young woman as she described her father's death, and the sparkle of merriment as one group described their first attempts to pick up boys, remain only in memory — although the tapes are still there to be listened to.

Inevitably in such a process I was intruding into private worlds, and was sometimes invited to comment and respond myself. To the boy who, first described his sexual education as being a process of 'trial and error — with a lot of errors and some pretty heavy trials!' and then asked me how I'd learnt, I had to admit to similar experiences. With the girl who wanted to just talk about the pain of her Mum and Dad's separation when she was ten, the interview was abandoned and forgotten. For the shop assistant who walked nearly a mile to show me the right bus stop, I hope the questions I answered about what she described as her 'boy friend's indifference' were some recompense for the walk back. An oft-expressed sentiment in these interviews is a criticism of adults who were just too busy to listen, and I could hardly ignore that judgment!

There were some beautiful moments.

Sitting on a sea wall in Port Isaac a soft Cornish voice expressed surprise that we'd been there for forty minutes. 'No one's ever got me to talk for that long.' In one town taking a group out for a drink as a break from interviewing, I was regaled by true-life stories involving Catholic priests and family arguments that made Billy Connolly sound more like the Pope. In Birmingham a lad had walked five miles and was sorry he'd kept me waiting, but he hadn't been able to afford the bus fare that day. He rejected my offer of recompense: 'I don't want to turn professional yet — they might stop me dole money!' In Big Lamp

Youth Club initial suspicion melted away when they realised I wasn't actually associated with the police and the toughest lad there, who'd done two years' 'porridge' for assault, fought off the others to carry my case to the taxi waiting outside in the drizzle when I left.

Most of them were surprised that anyone thought they'd have anything worth recording but I was delighted how well they interviewed. I felt that I was more nervous than they were and I understood, for the first time, the Michael Parkinson nose-rubbing syndrome. It was encouraging to discover how interested they all were in discussing and reflecting, how optimistic the majority of them were, and how more than half had enjoyed school, despite all their criticisms. But I was saddened to find some articulate and determined young people still on the dole two or three years after leaving school, having spent a very fruitless, rootless and meaningless start to 'adult life'. After seventy interviews I am left with some general impressions that stick in my mind.

Although most of them had left school with little prospect of further education or a satisfying job, all of them had interests, skills and perceptions that left me wondering at the waste of ability. For whatever reason a vast, untapped resource of human potential seems to pass through our schools unrecognised. With one exception none of these young people interviewed wanted to be on the dole, yet most had experienced long periods of unemployment.

The life of the lazy and the indulged (mostly to be found at Monte Carlo or on Mediterranean yachts) was *not* something they yearned for. They wanted to work, not just for the money but for the self-esteem and purpose they felt a job could give. Their worry and depression about living in a world of uncertain work (cushioned by semi-satisfying YOP schemes), showed through in every case, but most were more resigned than bitter. 'It's how things are, you can't change 'em', expressed a common sentiment.

Though we work with young people who tend to be critical of school — as those of you who have read *In and Out of School* and *Absent with Cause* will know — I was surprised at how consistently perceptive they were about the processes going on within school. Although some of their comments were echoes of phrases I have heard many times from school leavers and simply confirmed my own preconceptions, other comments struck new chords and made me stop and think. I was surprised to have my preconceptions contradicted so flatly by their responses to certain questions, and for me those were the most valuable comments. We hope that their comments make you stop and think too.

Chapter 1

Primary school and transition to secondary

Part 1 — Primary school

'It's good, can I come again?'

I remember the first morning, 'cos me Mum came in and said, 'Come on you've got to go to school.' I said, 'Alright, I'll try it — do I have to go back if I don't like it?' And she said, 'You've got to go there for quite a long time.' I went up there and went into the classroom. I remember the other kids crying, but I don't remember myself crying. It was just a room with a whole load of desks in it. I thought, 'What the heck have I let myself in for?'

Andrew Pearce, aged 16, St Austell, Cornwall

My Mum says that after my first day I said, 'It's good, can I come again?' So I must have liked it, although I just remember a lot of playing with toys and the day always seemed to be too long for me.

Robert Morris, aged 17, Sutton Coldfield, West Midlands

You relax more as you go through primary school. In the fourth year you sort of run things. You get more out of play times. We always played football in the play times but we didn't in the first year because all the bigger kids would nick the ball.

I had one teacher I got on well with. She'd take an interest in us as we were going home; she'd come up and ask us where we were going and what we were going to do that night.

Andrew Seal, aged 19, Grear Barr, Birmingham

It really hit me coming from infants' school where I'd had women teachers all the time, to junior school where we had a Mr Prior, and I was scared stiff of my first male teacher. I was really worried and I

9

cried for about two weeks before I had to go. When I got there he was old and a bit boring but in a friendly sort of way, and I really enjoyed that year. I don't think I've ever enjoyed school as much as I did that one. He was a lot like my Dad except that my Dad's very strict, and Mr Prior had this soft spot. My Dad hasn't many soft spots!

Cheryl Davidson, aged 17, Bretton, Peterborough

'Parents should be involved with their kids'

I was hardly ever at primary school. My Mother was never happy unless there was something seriously wrong with me – she was that sort of hypochondriac. She used to send notes saying I was ill, to excuse me from sports, but really she couldn't afford the PE gear! She said I had a suspected hole in my heart! The teacher would say, 'Oh yes, OK that's fine, take your time and walk slowly round the park.'

Primary school was quite an old building. There wasn't really a playing field; it was more like concrete, in Govan, near the shipyards. There were about fifty in each class so that no teacher had any time for an individual pupil. If you'd got a problem, then that was hard luck. But one of the teachers was pretty young, called Miss Gray. She was understanding. One day I came into school late and as I was getting into gym gear she noticed a few bruises on me, and said, 'Where did you get those bruises?' 'Oh – I fell.' She asked if my Mother had been hitting me. 'No! Not my Mother, she wouldn't hit me.' So she made me strip off to the waist and I was covered in a few more bruises and she called in the Headmaster and the First Aid woman and the Headmaster told me to strip completely and my balls were bruised. The teacher said, 'You didn't get that in a fall.' I said I'd been in a fight. 'You weren't in a fight because I saw you go home last night and you weren't in a fight.' 'I was in a fight later when I got home!' She asked if my Mother had hit me. 'My Mother wouldn't dare hit me!' The Headmaster got on to the social workers to arrange a holiday for me for a few months to get away from my Mother, 'cos he knew she'd given me the bruises. If I'd said yeah, and they'd tackled her about it, I probably wouldn't be alive now. I don't think she could control herself. She used to get into a temper for no apparent reason.

I used to do sewing classes, like sewing up rag dolls and things. I couldn't concentrate on reading and writing, because when I was away from my Mother it was such a relief, that I could only be interested in lessons for a few hours and then as the day went on I started thinking about what was going to happen at home again. So I never really had much time to think about school. I suppose people tried to teach me to read and write, but I just couldn't find the way. I learnt to tell the time.

They had a big clock on the wall and they just used to ask at random what time it was. I was telling the time when I was about seven or eight. I think I was reasonably clever then.

In the first year of school I tore a little girl's dress on the school gate. I was swinging on it. It was winter but she was wearing a flimsy summer dress and I caught her dress and tore it, and the Head marched me straight in the office and gave me six of the belt. Even in Glasgow, no one gets six of the belt unless they're really bad, and then not usually till they're nine or ten, but I copped it when I was six. I went home to tell my Mother and she came up and nearly killed the Headmaster; they had to get two janitors to pull her off him. She was concerned when it came to *other* people belting me.

I don't blame my primary school because I can't read or write very well. I blame my upbringing – the atmospheric pressures around me – worrying about my Mother particularly. I never really thought even a week ahead. What's going to happen today was the main thing. If I could get through the day without too much bother then that was good.

My Mother wasn't interested in me and she didn't take any interest in the house at all. She was interested in going round the neighbours. Any guy that took her fancy she would go off with for so many months until he got sick of her. My Father was at work; he would come home, then go out to a church service most nights of the week. After a while I began to realise that my Mother wasn't interested, my Father wasn't interested 'cos he'd got his work and went to his church, so I took off and made my own life outside. Even when my Father said, 'Look you're doing bad at school,' I'd say, 'Why are you bothered; you haven't bothered before?' You don't want to stay at home and do homework because you feel no one's interested. I had a friend called Kenneth. His parents were interested from the day he was born. When he went to primary school and came home, he'd change into old clothes and they would sit with him and do an hour's work writing a passage out of the Bible or a newspaper – didn't really matter what it was from – as long as he wrote a paragraph, and then they gave him a dozen sums from the kind of sums he was doing, and they would have a game at night. Mother and Father sitting there. Parents should be involved with their kids.

Gordon MacMillan, aged 23, Baptist Mills, Bristol

It was good – we had a big playground and my Mother was cook there. When I used to beat up the boys, she used to beat me up. I went to a number of primary schools because they kept closing soon after I started.

Carl Benjamin, aged 20, Easton, Bristol

11

Young people's comments

I was labelled dyslexic right from the start and they tried tae put me in a mentally handicapped school. It was only because my Mum and Dad fought for me (saying there was nothing *that* wrong with me) that they allowed me intae a 'normal' school; but even there they split me off and made me go intae a reading unit. Right until secondary school I was always something special in the class, because I'd be taken out for an hour every day.

Maureen McLaughlin, aged 18, Edinburgh

'The people doing best were near the front'

I remember in my last year at primary school the teacher tended to arrange the desks so that the people doing best were near the front, going back to the ones who weren't doing very well, which I thought was a bit bad. It made you think you had to get on to the next desk and you got all upset about it. I was in the middle.

I never really *thought* about things. You're not mature enough to take any notice. You just go along with it.

Ley Alberici, aged 17, Great Barr, Birmingham

My little niece, who's five, came home the other day. She's just started school and what she said upset me. 'If we done a good piece of work we get gold stars, but you know something Mandy, the teacher sticks it on your head. I wish they wouldn't do that.' I said, 'Don't you tell the teacher?' 'No,' she says, 'I wouldn't do that.' But the poor kid doesn't want a gold star stuck on her head! It's pathetic, it's degrading.

Mandy Smith, aged 19, Withywood, Bristol

My Mum didn't like it when we had to write out a list of what presents we'd had at Christmas time, because she thought kids would compete with what they'd got. So she complained to the teacher – who was often rude to me after that. She had favourites in the class and I wasn't one of them. I was getting really upset there and my Mum heard about the Durdham Park free school and thought it would do me good to go to a different school – that it would open me up a bit. So I went there. We didn't learn much but it did me good. There wasn't set lessons; you'd go in and do what you like; you'd do yoga in the library; we'd go canoeing, ice skating, look after animals and make shampoo in the science lab. I learnt a lot, but it wasn't like what you learn in schools. It wasn't anything that would help me in a CSE but it was something that'd help me in life – the difference between learning to meditate and cope, and learning when Henry VIII died.

When I went back to ordinary primary school after Durdham Park,

12

the kids really looked down their noses at me. They said you didn't learn anything there, you didn't have any lessons. When I told them what we used to do I was really considered low. I always felt like the dunce of the class. There was one girl on at me all the time for going to Durdham Park School. 'You were only playing with chickens all day,' she said, but I enjoyed it. I felt like I learnt a hell of a lot there, but it was nothing I could write down on paper. It was things like confidence and self-expression. It was your choice to go in when you wanted and you didn't *have* to do art. Mind you, there were things I should have been learning like maths which went to pot. Because I didn't like it I didn't go, but now I think I should have. Choice *is* important but it has its problems. Subjects that you're not strong at which are quite still important, you may just lose altogether.

Jemma Littlefair, aged 17, St Werburgh's, Bristol

At primary school you do nearly the same things as at home, like playing with bricks or cars. I wanted to do different things. I hated milk and they used to make you drink those quarter-pint things. In winter it was hard and cold and in summer it was warm, with a sickly smell. I've never liked milk ever since then.

It was frightening to start with, because you never knew anybody and you didn't know what to expect. I was sent to a convent school and the nuns were very strict. They'd rap your knuckles with a ruler. They seemed so big to start with, although as you grew older they seemed to get smaller.

Marcel Rosari, aged 18, St Austell, Cornwall

I hated primary school. I couldn't spell, my desk was a mess and I was bad at arithmetic, which seemed the main subject that primary school was based on. Even in art I'd be in trouble for making a mess, because I'd end up with paint all over me.

Yvonne Gray, aged 19, Marchmont, Edinburgh

Part 2 – Juniors to seniors

'It was better than I thought it was going to be'

I didn't look forward to going. The one I went to had a bad reputation; all the lads who went there were supposed to be bullies, and me and my mates were really worried about going. It seemed massive compared to the other school. Primary school had about ten classrooms, but this one had fifty or sixty rooms. There were thousands of pupils compared to the two hundred at primary school. I felt lonely. Primary school was like a little community. Secondary schools seemed so large, but it was better than I thought it was going to be.

Robert Morris, aged 17, Sutton Coldfield, West Midlands

I enjoyed secondary more than primary because at primary school you just sat in one class all day with the same teacher, which was boring. In secondary school I hated it at first, when you had to change classes all the time, but really it's much better, 'cos when you leave school you're going tae meet a lot of people. Meeting different teachers and sussing them out helps you when you leave school tae suss other people out. But when you have the same teacher all year you get that used tae her and that bored of her voice that you know what she's going tae say next.

Jayne Harper, aged 16, Edinburgh

In primary school you behave because you're younger, but in secondary school you find out that other people are getting away with things so you try it on too; 'I forgot to do my homework', or 'I couldn't make the lesson because I had a dentist's appointment'. But the teachers were the same really. If you were nice to them they were nice to you.

Kristine King, aged 18, Bretton, Peterborough

I was getting neat grades at primary school. Then I moved up to Castle Secondary. I didn't like it for the first week or so. I wasn't used to wearing uniform, but the first year at secondary you were treated as though you were a lot older. The school was run differently too: you had to move around different classes in between lessons. You had to move from one block to another and, when it was raining, you'd walk into a class really downhearted. Whereas you were just in one room in junior school getting different lessons all the time.

Alan Myserscough, aged 20, Lancaster

It's scary for the first week. I thought I'd be with my friends from middle school but we were split up. When you get to know people and you get to know teachers it's great, because you find a whole new circle of friends, so you've got your friends at home as well as at school.

Brian Carr, aged 17, Forest Hill, Newcastle-upon-Tyne

I felt grown-up moving from primary to secondary, but I was very nervous. In fact I fainted on my first day. It was very hot and I had my new uniform on. We were being welcomed by the Headmistress and everything went fuzzy.

Audrey Nelson, aged 18, Edinburgh

'There's a tremendous distance between you and the teachers'

There was a load of difference. When you were in junior school, the teachers would come and sit by you. They'd watch you writing and they'd have discussions with you. In secondary school they just didn't involve themselves like that.

They don't really teach you in the seniors. All they thought about was putting the work up on the board, telling you to get it into the book and that was it. That'd be the lesson over.

John Masefield, aged 19, Kingstanding, Birmingham

The worst part of it was changing to go to a higher school. That was the most difficult, because you had to change classes and teachers. In primary school you get addicted to one teacher. You can say, 'Right, I'll see so and so tomorrow'; same old thing every day. But in higher school there are so many different rooms, so many different people and so many kids. It's like going to Wembley I suppose. If you need help, if something's difficult, or a load of people ask you a question and you don't know, they start giving you the elbow and start taking the piss. You get called all sorts of names if you have trouble and can't do it. You have to keep calling the teacher backwards and forwards. Then the teacher says, 'How many times have I been through this with you? You should know it,' and you get agitated.

The worst part was going into a class full of complete strangers. When I went to me first class I never knew no one. Some kid said something and I reared up and that was when I realised I was going to be a loser, because they'd all been in the class together for some time.

Matthew Brown, aged 17, Chelmsford, Essex

It was a tremendous change moving from primary to secondary. There were so many more people and life was that bit more complex. Before I went to Bodmin Comprehensive most of my teachers were on friendly terms with me, but when you get to comprehensive there's a tremendous distance between you and the teachers.

Barrie McGovern, aged 21, Bodmin, Cornwall

When I took my IQ test at secondary school they put me in the class just above the remedial group. It was a really rough area and they gathered us all together in one class and gave us hulking teachers — like ex-rugby players and karate experts. They didn't hassle us too much because, if they started picking on someone, we'd say, 'Fuckin' well leave him alone!'

We had a reputation the day we started secondary school. By twelve we could beat grown-up guys and by the time we were thirteen or fourteen we were flicking knives at each other. You had to be violent to survive.

'Tory Crimes', aged 18, Glasgow

'I went to senior school and everything stopped'

You don't learn as much as in the juniors, 'cos you're pampered in the juniors so you're willing to work. But once you're in a comprehensive you're growing up faster and you don't want to listen.

Martin Yates, aged 18, Kingstanding, Birmingham

I loved primary school. I wanted to be a school teacher when I was at that school — I loved it so much — but it all changed when I went to secondary. Round here you take your eleven plus if you're within a certain radius of Matlock — three miles I think. We automatically went to Wirksworth. There was one exception — a girl whose Father knew the Headmaster of Baileys — which made me mad, because I thought I'd be able to go to Baileys and I wanted to. I thought I'd have got on better. When I went up to Wirksworth they didn't seem to care as much about individuals. There were certain teachers who liked you and that, but they cared more about the really clever ones who were going to university.

The trouble is you make a lot of friends at primary school and then they split you up. I still see them to say 'Hello' to, but we used to be really friendly. At primary school I was amongst the top people — clever I suppose you'd call it. But I can remember the first maths test we had at secondary school I was near the bottom, which really upset me and I don't think I bothered after that. I was only eleven, and up 'till then I thought I'd be something. In the end I didn't even pass maths O level although I'd been top in it at primary school.

Janet Gould, aged 17, Bonsall, Derbyshire

My best friend went to a different school and I was split up from my other friends, because we were put in classes according to how clever we were. I was in the top class but I never fitted in because I still went around with my old friends at play time — so I was sort of singled out by people in my class. The really clever ones I didn't speak to at all. I was sent to Child Guidance in my first year, because they said I didn't like going to school. But I *did* go to school — I never knocked off — it was just that I didn't work enough in school. I thought it was silly going to Child Guidance. I couldn't understand why I was going and nobody explained it to me. I used to tell my friends I was just having the day off. I didn't dare tell them where I was going.

16

I still don't understand it. I was enjoying myself in the juniors and then I went to senior school and everything stopped. I suddenly didn't want to go to school. In the juniors I was reading books and everything.

Andrew Seal, aged 19, Great Barr, Birmingham

I was fairly bright for me age at primary school, but when I got to secondary school it all changed. People just didn't seem to want to go after the first year or so. I had quite a few friends, but they were all the wrong sort and I ended up not going to school very often. When I did go back everyone was miles ahead of me, which just made things worse. The only things I really enjoyed were break times and dinner times. Teachers didn't seem to notice whether I was there or not, which was another reason for not bothering to go in. If I was on report and missed a day I could still get away with saying, 'You forgot to sign my report yesterday' and they'd sign it 'cos they didn't know I wasn't there.

I reckon I learnt most when I was in primary school and during my first and second years at secondary school.

Joanne Clark, aged 17, Chelmsford, Essex

'Maybe I was a washout'

When you went to secondary school for the first day a big gang of kids would come round you and knock the shit out of you and up till I left school that was the sort of ruling of the school. You got your trousers or jumper ripped as some sort of initiation to the school, and for me it was a good kicking as well.

I think I was a complete write-off in terms of subjects. I couldn't write, so I felt embarrassed that people would laugh if they saw that an eleven-year-old couldn't write as well as a five-year-old.

There was a special class in the school and they tried quite hard to help me, but I think I needed someone to push me more than they were prepared to. Maybe they thought if they pushed me too hard I would leave or go off. It wasn't so much school that was a washout. Maybe *I* was a washout. Maybe the school wasn't at fault. Perhaps it was *me*.

Gordon MacMillan, aged 23, Baptist Mills, Bristol

See pp. 110-15 for the response by Neville Bennett.

Chapter 2

Secondary school

'Communication is very, very important'

Schools ought to teach you how to cope with life when you leave school. Of course, you need exams because people want to go to Universities and colleges, so you can't just take them away, but you should have other things, so that when you leave school you know how to sign on, you know how to write a letter for a job, you know what to say in an interview; when you find a flat you know how to deal with the landlord, you know how to pay your rent money; if a tap starts leaking you know how to mend it, you know what sort of food to buy, and how to cook proper meals. A lot of kids just haven't a clue how to do any of those.

Schools need to do more of these things, but when you start secondary school and you're in a group of thirty people you don't even talk amongst each other. You're with the same group for three or four years yet you hardly know any of them. A girl comes in with loads of makeup and disco sort of clothes, and you see the person, but you don't know what she's like underneath. If you could get to know your group and understand them and share things about yourself with them, then you know that you have friends you can share problems with. If kids can go into school feeling that they're not alone, feeling that they're not the only person with problems, that there are people that do understand, people that care, then that's one barrier broken down immediately. I'm not saying that everybody has problems but quite a lot of kids do have.

It ought to start as soon as you go into school. You can't teach people to be understanding but you can give them the opportunity to learn to be, by putting them in situations where they learn naturally. Give them different people's problems. Let them express their own feelings about it and what they'd do if they were in the same situation. I don't think you can invent problems; you have to talk about real problems.

Communication is very, very important. For people who are very shy you can't teach it, but you can have groups talking and things like that, to help them come out of themselves. At the moment in schools there's hardly any real communication at all. You have a staff room for all the teachers while the kids are just shoved out in the playground. There's no communication once the forty-minute lesson's over. But in normal circumstances after forty minutes with friends you don't just switch off and say, 'That's that; we've been talking for forty minutes and we're not talking any more.' Talking is one way of breaking down prejudices, like between black and white. If you can encourage black people to talk *with* whites, tell them about themselves so that the whites get to know them, you can begin to break down the prejudice that their parents have drummed into them.

The trouble is it needs schools to be more open places but they tend to teach you to be competitive. You're not really taught to share, but when you leave school and live with someone you *have* to share. Being taught to keep things to yourself, like saying 'This is my work, you can't copy it' doesn't help you. Doing things in groups would make it better. People say it's not natural to share things, but if you're married you're sharing with the person you're married to. Anyway people do share a lot of things — like shops and roads, for example!

It'd be difficult to do all this though because in one class you've got people of different levels of maturity. You find some sixteen-year-olds who are just the same as twelve-year-olds, and some twelve-year-olds who are like sixteen-year-olds. It would be hard for some of them to cope with the freedom of a more open place, but then freedom is something people have to learn how to handle.

You can't always do what you want, even when you've left school. You have to learn that the limits come when you start affecting other people. Freedom is not just within yourself if you're involved with other people. It's something you can only work out as a group, and schools could help you to learn this.

Jo Chadwick, aged 17, Trowbridge, Wilts

You can't put up your hand and say, 'Sir, this lesson's very boring.' You just aren't allowed to do that in school. If you feel it's boring, you think there's something wrong with *you*; you get worried because everybody else is writing things down. Everybody else is telling you what's best for you and what ain't, but you're never taught to question anything. You're never taught to think like that. If you do question anything, there's something wrong with you: you're insolent, you're naughty, you're a thug. I remember once being so bored with geology

19

that I started reading my book, *Fantastic Mr Fox*, and the teacher called me out. 'Mandy, what are you doing?' 'I'm reading *Fantastic Mr Fox.*' He told me to get out. When I said, 'Actually I find your lesson very boring,' he thumped me and sent me to the Deputy Head. He could at least have took it that I found the lesson very boring.

Mandy Smith, aged 19, Withywood, Bristol

'I'd expand the form representative system'

The one consolation in our school was having year representatives. I was chosen for my form, probably because I was a bit out of the ordinary, having a motor bike. If anyone in the form had a query for the teachers it went through me. At the meeting the Deputy Head would have all our proposals on a bit of paper. For example 'Why do we have to queue up for dinner in the middle of the playground, with footballs flying everywhere?' So it was decided we'd go through the other entrance. Once, we decided on a mufti day, when kids could come in whatever clothes they wanted. It cost 5p for the day and the money went to charity. But if you were discussing queries like a teacher sending someone out of the class, the Deputy Head would always say that the teacher was only doing his job.

Ley Alberici, aged 17, Great Barr, Birmingham

I was a year representative for the School Council once. How it worked was that the class representative took issues tae the year representative who took it tae the Head Girl or Head Boy, who both sat at the Council meeting with sixty teachers, the priest and the Headmistress. But tae have just two people sitting on the Council was a token: two members for 1,200 pupils! The Head Girl and Head Boy had been hand-picked by the rector in any case. There were ten candidates put forward by the teachers and they chose the one who went tae church on Sunday and worked in the Smiley Club.

Mary Seath, aged 17, Edinburgh

I'd expand the form representative system. In my school we had meetings with the Headmaster every fortnight and at least it meant the Head wasn't a million miles away. Kids could be given more say in some things – like trips away or what to do in PE lessons. They need to feel involved.

Schools get it right in the sixth form by allowing them to vote about their own uniform, elect their own Head Boy, set up their own committees, but they should bring that in in stages from the second or third year. Most thirteen-year-olds don't make it to the sixth form and don't

20

get used to making decisions – yet two years after leaving school they can vote. Somehow they have to get used to making decisions.

Youth clubs could help out in this way. They should be more than just leisure centres. With their relaxed atmosphere they could take a more active role in teaching kids decision-making. Schools can't cover everything from nine to three-thirty.

Leslie Howie, aged 17, Wallsend, Tyne and Wear

I was on the School Council for a time, but I gave it up, because if you put something forward it was nearly always ignored. We'd ask for the clocks to be repaired, and they'd say no, it couldn't be afforded. Some-one had taken the locks off the toilet doors so that they wouldn't stay shut and we'd ask for them to be repaired, but no, it couldn't be afford-ed. Yet when they were doing a school production of *Oliver*, we had to sign contracts saying we wouldn't skive off rehearsals because they were spending so much on it. It seemed an awful lot considering we'd been told we couldn't afford any more books. So we put a question to the School Council asking whether they should be allowed to spend that much, since they didn't *need* to have that many fancy lights. The girl who brought it up was hauled in front of the Deputy, who was pro-ducing the show, and he told her it was nothing to do with the School Council.

Yvonne Gray, aged 19, Marchmont, Edinburgh

You're supposed tae elect someone tae represent your year, but it's a fix, because it's always the person the teacher wants. You vote but the votes are counted away from the pupils and the most disliked person in the class often seems tae be the representative! If you said you wanted tae see the votes counted in front of everybody they'd say 'That's just sour grapes because you weren't picked.' You know that behind your back they're saying, 'Miss McLaughlin is a political activist and if we ever had her on the School Council it would just be a shambles.' If you really did have a democratic school council it would make a lot of dif-ference.

Teachers say that pupils are too irresponsible tae run anything, but they don't give pupils a chance tae try. I doubt whether pupils would actually be irresponsible, because if you had tae run something you'd want tae make it work and not make a fool of yourself.

Maureen McLaughlin, aged 18, Edinburgh

'It's easy to become a book'

Schools should teach you to realise yourself, but they don't. They teach you to be a book. It's easy to become a book, but to become yourself you've got to be given various choices and be helped to look at the choices. You've got to learn that, otherwise you're not prepared for the outside world.

I wouldn't say just do what you want. I'd go into a class, tell them what they've got to learn, and what's important, and then let the kids choose their timetable for the week. As long as you make it look like the kids are doing something towards the school, it makes it harder for the kids to complain. So I'd get them together at the beginning of term to decide when they want this lesson and that lesson. Perhaps you don't have games on Thursday morning in the winter when you know it's going to be freezing cold, or maths last two on Friday in the summer when you're not going to learn nothing.

That way you learn about democracy don't you? You can't please everybody but you can please the majority of the class. As you move up each year you could give the kids more control gradually. When it comes to third years, for instance, a kid should be able to look back over the previous two years and say, 'I'm bad at this, or this', and get proper advice. They're going to say that certain kids are going to take advantage of this, but a lot of kids take advantage of the system anyway now — more than should — and more than would in this system I think.

Ray Scanlon, aged 17, Lawrence Weston, Bristol

I mucked about in the third and fourth years and when the time came for the prefects to be picked out me name came up and I thought, 'How the heck did I get into this? I've been a trouble maker all the time teasing prefects and mucking around.'

It made me behave better. I didn't think it would, but I had to set an example or I wouldn't be respected by the ones I had to keep under control. Trying to get eleven- and twelve-year-olds to do what you say is pretty difficult. I made friends with most of them, and then they would do as I said. The first couple of weeks when I went into the classroom and had to look after them during wet break I said, 'Right you lot, I'm your new prefect' and most of them made friends with me within the first two months. They'd hear one of me mates calling me 'Andrew' and they'd come up to me and say, 'Hi And, my name's so and so.' If you're friendly to them they're friendly to you.

Andrew Pearce, aged 16, St Austell, Cornwall

I think schools could do a lot to bring out a person's character. If a kid's caught stealing, the school should take them aside and have a chat with them, not bollock them or ram the law down his throat, but explain that if they steal a couple of Mars Bars from a shop the shopkeeper has to pay for those Mars Bars. Knowing right from wrong is important.

Some people say they wouldn't steal from a *shop* but if they walked along the road and saw a guy drop ten pounds they'd pick it up and put it in their pocket. That's wrong because it's still theft. I think personally if I saw a person drop money, whether he's in a Rolls-Royce or walking to work, I'd still say, 'Excuse me mate, you've dropped money.' I've got a bad conscience. If I picked up a penny in the street I'd be looking to see if someone was going to point their finger at me!

Keeping my word is very important to me as well. It's probably because I've been let down a lot so that if I let someone down I know what they're going to feel like. I try my best not to let someone down.

Gordon MacMillan, aged 23, Baptist Mills, Bristol

Obviously you need a certain amount of discipline, otherwise everything's going to go to pieces, and it must be hard to draw the borderline between discipline and relaxation. More consultation with the kids would be better, because a lot of decisions are made just by teachers and they do affect the pupils. Teachers think pupils aren't old enough, but most of them are really, and some are older than the teachers in some ways. Perhaps having a body of pupils who could speak to staff meetings would help.

Geoff Clark, aged 18, Bodmin, Cornwall

A lot of teachers disagree with some of the things that go on in school. For instance, I was once told off for wearing daps and jeans, and I said to the teacher, 'All right, but I'm not going to change, just because the rules say you want me to.' And she replied, 'I agree with you, I think kids ought to be able to wear what they want to, but because I'm here and the school governors have fixed these rules, then I've got to abide by it.' She said there were other teachers who felt the same way. So why can't they do something about it? It seems to me that it's just the people at the top of the school, the people who don't actually work there, who have all the say in things that go on in schools. I think schools ought to be run by the pupils and teachers together.

Kids have got to learn responsibility somewhere and that's a good way to start. It wouldn't turn into chaos if you've got teachers there to say 'no' to things like a ten-year-old saying, 'We want to be able to smoke.' Kids should have a say in things that are going to affect them — not teachers' salaries, but subjects, uniform, rules.

Jo Chadwick, aged 17, Trowbridge, Wilts

When I was suspended I had to gang see a wife for two hours a day. They wouldn't have me back at the school 'cos I'd give it a bad name. I would've liked to stay at school to do metalwork and woodwork but most of the teachers were awful — except for English. We had two

23

teachers for English. One was a wife and she was the best one. You could talk in her class and you'd still do your work. The other teacher would say, 'Shurrup, when I want you to talk I'll open the lid for the bin.' Teachers like posh kids more, and when it came to swimming these were the classes that went.

John Thompson, aged 16, Elswick, Newcastle-upon-Tyne

'Schools will always be somewhere that some people never like'

I was in the top year all the way through because it was a new school, and we grew up as the school grew up. The teachers treated us as the oldest all the time: they'd give us responsibilities and, because you were the oldest, you'd accept that responsibility — like going on the door at school discos or helping to sell raffle tickets. If you feel involved you're bound to feel it's a better place. But I think school will always be somewhere that some people never like. I don't think it's possible to do something in every school so that everyone in the school will always like it.

Kristine King, aged 18, Bretton, Peterborough

Some people don't like school, 'cos it's so rigid. You start at 9.00 a.m. and leave at 3.30 p.m. You have to do it every day from Monday to Friday. Your only days off are Saturday and Sunday. But it'll be exactly the same when they start work except that you get paid for going to work, and you don't get paid for going to school.

Tracy Atkinson, aged 16, Longbenton, Newcastle-upon-Tyne

I hated school. It was run by priests. All the kids round here are catholics. I was suspended several times and I was in and out of detention. The only thing I'd suggest to improve it is to blow it up. There were one or two teachers I liked — they used to *ask* you to do things and the rest would *tell* us to do things. They would say please and show us some politeness. Instead of saying, '*You* get the ruler now' they'd say, 'Oh Sean, can you get the ruler please?'

Sean Cross, aged 16, Elswick, Newcastle-upon-Tyne

I enjoyed school until I came to the fourth year. Then they piled too much homework on you. I'd do it, but I'd do it as quick as I could, and get it out the way. I used to hate school most of the time, but I didn't miss lessons, because of my parents really. I didn't know why we were doing some things. The teachers said it would help us pass an exam, but they've been no real use to me. I think we should have been taught what we need to know about when you *do* leave school.

Catherine Crowe, aged 17, Wardley, West Midlands

School was all right to start with in my first year, but once they got to know me it became worse. I was fed up with people taking the piss out of me and I didn't like going just because of this. My social worker thought I was making excuses. People think that nothing happens to kids what happens to grown ups. If I say I'm depressed people think that I don't know what the word means. I think schools should be tougher on the big kids who set on little people like me. You get fed up being picked on, so you stay away from school, which makes it worse. But it's not really your fault — it's the fault of the people making you stay away.

> Wayne Landsown, aged 19, Knowle West, Bristol

If you were walking along the corridor and you heard a bell you were supposed to go down on your knees. One day, I was reading a book in the corridor when I heard the bell. The priest came walking up and he said, 'Kneel.' I said, 'What?' He said, 'Kneel!' I said, 'Who do you think you are? King Arthur?' I was suspended for that.

> Stephen Rice, aged 16, Elswick, Newcastle-upon-Tyne

It was the last school I was at when I began to realise you could do other things instead of just going to school. I used to be in the rock'n' roll society. I went to all the clubs and the dances and began to meet friends instead of going to school. I'd be with the Teddy boys and Teddy girls. It was much better than maths.

> Beverley Fenwick, aged 17, Whitley Bay, Northumberland

Every school has its bad points. The bad one in ours was the building.

I was thinking I was going to college till they showed us round and it seemed worse than school.

> Catherine Crowe, aged 17, Wardley, West Midlands

I've been to four secondary schools — three all-girls' schools, and one mixed. The mixed school was the worst. In an all-girls' school the girls act themselves, but in the mixed school they all seemed to be so conscious that there were boys there — fashion-conscious for instance. When you mix boys and girls they seem to be trying to impress each other, and are more interested in that than learning anything. Of course, it's important to learn about the opposite sex, but you don't need to go to school with boys to do that, because you do see them at other times. In my case my brother used to bring his friends home and I would relate to them easily enough. I reckon if you find it difficult to relate to boys in a girls' school you'll find it just as difficult to relate in a mixed school.

You get on much faster with what you're learning in a girls' school.

You don't have boys looking over your shoulder thinking 'She's nice.' I reckon boys in a girls' school are a real put off.

Caroline Asquith, aged 16, Easton, Bristol

'I went to school just to meet my mates'

It wasn't totally useless going to school, because if you don't have any education you'd end up being scared to talk to people. Going to school helps because you've got to meet people. Even if that's the only use for it, that's probably a good thing.

Phil Bird, aged 21, Hartcliffe, Bristol

I went to school just to meet my mates really. It was the free time I enjoyed mostly. I suppose I would have met them in town, but truancy wasn't something I was into. The trouble with me was that I was quite easily led and I got in with the wrong people as soon as I started school.

Mark Baker, aged 19, Bretton, Peterborough

It's boring not being at school, but it seemed *more* boring being at school. At least when I wasn't at school I wasn't on my own. We used to sit in Toak's — a café in town — but they got fed up with having school kids in there because it began to look like a school. In the end they said, 'If you're coming in here you've got to spend at least 25p,' which finished it really 'cos we'd been used to buying tea at 23p and making it last all morning. It was ever so boring though.

Joanne Clark, aged 17, Chelmsford, Essex

The problem with a lot of kids today is that they haven't worked out who they are; they just want to belong to a visible group. They think they have an identity because they belong to a group. When I was at school, I felt more secure within a group. Nobody would ever challenge me, ask me, 'Who are *you*?'

'Tory Crimes', aged 18, Glasgow

'Kids who lark around are wasting time'

I think kids who lark around are wasting time. They're there and they've got to be educated whether they want to or not. If they don't then when they leave school they're going to realise, 'I knew I should have done that' and they'll look back and see they've made a big mistake. I do sometimes, like when I went for a job once and felt embarrassed that I didn't know how to do dividing. They took the form away and said, 'Thank you, that'll be all.' That was my job gone.

John Masefield, aged 19, Kingstanding, Birmingham

I'm stupid really for not thinking more about school at the time. I could have made much more of it. But I was a real yobbo then – the real McCoy, Jack the Crack. If I was in the corridor, they'd move out of my way. There were six of us who wore the same thing – badges, crombies, and Dr Martens. I can remember once a teacher tried to make me take off me Martens and walk around in me socks, but I wouldn't have none of that and I had a real barney with him. I was getting into a lot of trouble so the Head had me in the office one day and said, 'What do you think about going on work experience?' I said, 'Yeah.' They said, 'We've been talking to Mr Brooks, the groundsman, who's getting on a bit and wants someone to give him a hand. We'll give you two or three days to think about if you are prepared to give it a go.'

Well, of course, everything changed then, particularly the teachers' attitudes. They were much more friendly. They became like custard, rolling all over me! I was talking to one of them about it and he said, 'Well, you're working here now so you're one of us. You're classed as staff really 'cos you're the groundsman. If anything ever goes wrong in the classroom we sort it out and deal with it, if anything goes wrong in the grounds – kids doing things they shouldn't – then you sort it out. You're one of the staff.' It was like being in a completely different organisation. It was like I was another person, like Prince Charles!

When I took the groundsman job, my brother was really annoyed. He said, 'What are you learning? How far are you going to get marking out football pitches? You ain't learning nothing are you?' I said, 'I can't because I've got so far behind, it's just got to a stage where they can't teach me nothing. They won't teach me. They can't have three people on one book and one of the blokes about seven books behind.' It didn't occur to me until I was just about to leave that they were using me. I realised the groundsman was being paid £50 or £60 a week for sitting on his arse while I was doing all the work and I thought, 'I ain't getting nothing out of this.'

It suddenly dawned on me. I was getting all mucked up with chalk, my boots were in a mess, I was being drenched in the rain, and all I was getting was a cold, and 'Cheers, see you tomorrow.' That same night me brother reared up at me again and said, 'They're just using you as cheap labour,' and so I thought, 'Sod it' and jacked it in. I'd done it for nearly a year though. Three days later they had another kid out helping him.

Matthew Brown, aged 17, Chelmsford, Essex

27

I wish I'd not knocked off so much, but I didn't really enjoy school, although I got on well with some of the teachers. The best thing we did was Community Service in the fifth year when we had a chance to help at an Old People's Home. We had a whole day for it and we used to take them down for their dinner, bring them back and make their teas. It showed us something of what a job was like. There was one woman I used to get on right well with. She was ninety-eight. She used to say, 'Do you want to do some knitting with me?' And I'd say, 'No, I've got to get you cups of teas.' Then I'd sit there talking to her. She talked about how, when she was a child, her Nanna used to learn her to knit, and how she'd been doing it ever since. They used to be good things she knitted. She talked about her grandchildren mostly. When I made the tea she used to say, 'Don't put too much sugar in for me,' and if they had any cakes left from the night before I used to give one to her. One day, there were four bouquets sent for the Home and I put the nicest one in her room.

But she died and I was right upset. I'd have gone to her funeral, except I didn't know about it till too late. I'd like to do that sort of thing as a job.

My Mum was interested in what was happening at school; she'd often ask me if I wanted any help but I used to say, 'No, I'll do it myself.' My Dad just used to let me get on with it, but he died just as I started in the fifth year. He committed suicide. He took some tablets. He didn't talk about it. All he left was a letter in a drawer. It was to me Mum. He said, 'I'm sorry I've left you like this, but I had to do it – Love Pete.'

He used to come home cheerful as owt – and he didn't used to show if he was fed up. It looked as though he just took the tablets and wrote the letter and then got into bed. Me Mum was asleep. When she woke up he was all cold. She came into me bedroom and woke me and Janet up and said, 'I think your Dad's dead.' I had to go down and tell me brother but I just stood there. I couldn't speak at all. Me Mum came down and said, 'Have you told him?' and I said, 'No, I can't.' But I managed to ring me other brother up and told him Dad was dead. He said, 'He isn't?' and I said, 'Would I joke about a thing like that?' He came along to the funeral but we haven't seen him since.

The school knew what had happened, but they didn't talk to me about it. I felt like getting it out though and I used to talk about it to me mates. When he died I couldn't believe it. I wasn't hardly crying, but when the curtains closed at the cremation I broke me heart.

It's been hard on me Mum, 'cos she's got to do her job and then she's got to do the house out when she comes back. I can help her now I've left school, but I can't sign on till 30th September, so I can't give her any money. In the holidays I used to clean out the chip shop and I got

£3 for that which was summat to give me Mum.

Karen Myerscough, aged 17, Lancaster

If you stop treating children as children in primary school and treat them as kids they'd grow faster. If you stop treating kids as kids in secondary school and treat them as adults, with responsibility, they'd grow up faster. It's no good starting by treating them as children and then changing your attitude half-way through. How you approach people is what matters. When they do something wrong, don't go up and make an issue of it. Saying things like, 'Stand outside boy' or, 'Your parents'll hear of this,' only makes people embarrassed, and when they're embarrassed people get aggressive back and then you've created another problem. I began to hate a lot of teachers because they made me aggressive in this way. Kids don't like being shamed. If I could be taken back to the same age again, and someone said, 'Here's your second chance; you either go through life as you did before and make school a waste of time, or you use your head and try and make something of it, I think I would go into school and supply me own papers, own pens and bugger the rest of the class; I would fight for *my* education.

Gordon MacMillan, aged 23, Baptist Mills, Bristol

'I just couldn't concentrate at school because . . . '

We moved to Bristol and my Mum married the same day. Her new husband used to beat the hell out of her; he used to beat me and my sister too but my Mum didn't care; she said if she interfered it would be worse; he'd take it out on us even more. So she used to work nights while he went out drinking. I'd come home from school and do the shopping. Then she'd want to know why the washing up wasn't done, so I'd come home from school wash up *and* go shopping. Then she'd want to know why the floor wasn't clean, so I'd come home earlier, take a lesson off or something, just to make her happy. I didn't have time to do my homework. She didn't care; she never asked what my homework was like or my reports. I didn't take any home in the end and she didn't even notice. I used to come home in the afternoon and she wouldn't say anything. Sometimes she'd ask why I wasn't at school and I'd say something like, 'We've got English off this afternoon.'

I think because the school knew that my Mum had trouble at home, and knew that we were being beaten up, they let me get away with things. There were days when I wouldn't go in — weeks when I didn't go in towards the end — and no one said anything.

Jemma Littlefair, aged 17, St Werburgh's, Bristol

I left high school in the third year and went into a children's home. I was causing trouble at school and I was in trouble at home. My Mum's an alcoholic and my Dad lives with another woman who I don't get on with, so I had real problems at home. At first I lived with my Mum from when I was little 'till I was about six. Then I went to live with my Dad in Newcastle, and things went wrong from then. I used to love to go to school to get out of the way of home, and when the holidays came around, that's when I used to get into trouble. I hated being at home 'cos she had a daughter and a son of her own and I didn't get on with them very well. In the end I ran away to Middlesborough to my sister's and she arranged for me to be put in a home, which I wanted.

Now it's great. I go home for visits weekends and it's a lot better. I get on with them great now. It was probably 'cos I was living there all the time. I didn't like her and she didn't like me. I think we should have been away from each other for a bit. I've become more sensible now. At the time I don't think the teachers believed me when I told them what was going on. I think they just thought I was having them on.

Denise Hegyesi, aged 16, Whitley Bay, Northumberland

Things weren't going very well at home, which was affecting my schooling. It was really that my old man used to drink heavily and whenever I came home from school he'd just go on and on at me. Some of the teachers knew I had a problem but I didn't speak about it. I thought it wasn't that important to them, although when they found out they seemed to act more sympathetically — like the head of our house group used to pay for my outings, which I really thanked him for. I felt a bit stupid but I used to accept every time because I knew it was getting me away from my parents.

I just couldn't concentrate at school. The home thing was making me go into a little shell and though I tried to get out of that frame of mind, it was really difficult. I never used to like getting into arguments with kids at school because I had enough of it at home. In the end I went to the Citizen's Advice Bureau to see if there was anything they could do. I had to take time off from school to see various people in the Social Service department. The case went to court and they said it was a good idea that I went into care. I would have preferred a flat or a bedsit, but I wasn't old enough. So at fifteen I went into a Family Group Home. Things took a long time to improve at school though, because the home was five miles from my school. I used to get up early, catch two buses and it would take an hour and a half some days. I'd be really tired, and if I got in late the teachers would go on at me. I suppose I could have changed schools, but I didn't want to. They advised me not to, although now, looking back, I think it might have been better if I had, because I never took any exams. I failed in all the mocks, so I thought, Sod it — I'll leave as soon as I can and get a job' — which I did.

Chris Rich, aged 18, Easton, Bristol

In the first and second year I was with my friends, but they weren't as bright as me and were put intae different gradings. It was good because I could help them and I learned more by helping them. It was getting it intae my brain as well as teaching them. But in the third year I was put in a class with people I didnae know and I felt stupid asking them. That's where it went wrong for me. I would have much preferred tae stay with my friends and I'd have worked better being able tae talk with them. I think splitting friends up is unnecessary, especially using A, B and C grades. People in C grades must feel really stupid compared tae their friends who've been put intae A grades.

In the fourth and fifth year I didnae really like school except for break and dinner times. I used tae skive quite a lot, until I was put under supervision in the children's home where I am now.

This girl attacked me and she made it out that it was me that attacked her so I got the blame for it. I was done for assault and breach of the peace. I had this belt on with studs in it, 'cos I used tae be a punk, and they done me for possession of an offensive weapon as well. I had tae go in front of a panel. It makes you feel really low. There's five people who've never seen you before. I didnae get a chance tae say anything. They just said, 'You're getting put on supervision and you'll be in this Home for a certain time and after a while you'll come back here and we will decide what's happening tae you.'

They asked me what I thought about it, but before I could think, they were talking about something else. They didnae give me a chance tae say what I thought about being put in a Home. They were saying that I was a disturbed child. I only had my Gran there 'cos my Mother and Father are divorced and my Dad was in hospital. My Grannie never had a clue what was happening. You feel really stupid just sitting there as they talk. I was put under a social worker who sees me about once every year and she said I would only be in care for six weeks, but when I went tae my panel again they said, 'No, that wasnae right.' I was meant tae be out last month but my Father died, so they put it back tae November. They just muck you about and then they wonder why you're a disturbed child.

Jayne Harper, aged 16, Edinburgh

I was hardly at school so I never got reports. Either I'd no decent clothes to wear — shoes or trousers — or I just didn't go. It wasn't that we were poor, because my Dad was earning good money, but my Mum never spent a penny of it in the house. I don't know where it went. Presumably

31

she was treating her boy friends, because she was something like a prostitute. And she'd need to treat them, not the other way round. . . . you should see her! I had a friend Billy, whose Dad was a lamplighter, and he'd come round after I'd gone to school. At the time it seemed only natural that he should come round to put out the gas, but then I discovered that Billy's Mum was asking for a divorce because he was playing around with my Mother.

Gordon MacMillan, aged 23, Baptist Mills, Bristol

I was pregnant by the end of the third year, so I spent a lot of the fourth year away from school. When I went back to school some of the teachers were a bit shocked and obviously didn't want to know me. They'd say, 'Sit down and I'll bring your books round in a minute.' But my tutorial teacher was different. He asked me how things had been when I was pregnant and how I was coping.

I was worried about how the rest of the class were going to react when I went back. But I used to go to the youth club while I was pregnant and everybody would say they wanted to see the baby when she was born. When I went back to school everyone was just the same and used to say, 'How's the baby?' and things like that. If I had a day off school, I used to take her up sometimes to see me mates. They all loved her and wanted to take her home.

I didn't want to leave the baby, but I'd missed school really while I'd been pregnant. I'd had a home tutor for two hours every day, which was boring, so I was glad to get back into a class with other people. It was funny going back. I'd always wanted to work with kids and yet they said I couldn't do the child care exam, because I had an unfair advantage over the others in the group!

School could have been different but it must be hard for teachers to make it interesting, when they have to look after so many. Quite a few kids have problems like they've only got a Mum like I have, 'cos me Dad died nine years ago, or their Mum and Dad have split up. I think that half the reason why people skip school is that they've got problems at home, and don't feel there's anyone at school who really cares.

You see I never used to talk to my Mum if I had problems, and it would have helped me to have someone else to talk with. My Mum was a bit disappointed when she found out I was pregnant, but she's had nine kids of her own and loves kids. The social worker was saying that I should have the baby adopted, but my Mum said it should be up to me what I done. 'Do you want to keep her?' she asked, and I said, 'Yes.' She said, 'All right but you'll have to try and help me at work at weekends to help with the money.' All my family have stood by me like that.

When my little girl's older I'm going to try and talk to her and rather than say 'You shouldn't skip school' like me Mum did to me, I'll try and

explain to her why she should go to school, even though it's boring. I'll
try and mix her in with people of different ages, so she's not so shy
about meeting people. And I'll try and be involved with her school.
When they have parents' evenings I'll try and go to 'em and discuss with
the teachers that she doesn't get on with. Whenever my school had an
open evening my Mum never went. She'd say, 'Oh, it's all the same.'
But I'd rather go — especially if she did have problems. If she said a
teacher was picking on her, I wouldn't just go up and have a go at the
teacher. I'd discuss it with her and find out why — whether she'd been
naughty in the class, or whether she just didn't want to work, or
whether it was that they didn't hit it off.

Ronny Moore, aged 17, Southminster, Essex

See pp. 116-22 for the response by David Hargreaves.

Chapter 3

Curriculum issues

Part 1 – Process and content

'When you're in school it's a protected world'

I don't think it educates you in the total sense of the word. It may teach you how to find square roots and you might gain some O levels, but I don't think school makes you think any more logically and rationally, or gives you the ability to use your experience.

Matthew Fforde, aged 17, Easton, Bristol

Learning about Palmerston in 1870 is not going to prepare you for the outside world of today. The first thing I'd do is take everyone down the Job Centre and say, 'Look there's fifty jobs in here and three million unemployed out there.' You have to get them to face the fact that they'll almost certainly be on the dole for a while. It's difficult to tell people that they're going to be on the scrap heap at sixteen. But you can show them how to keep their minds occupied – sports centres and libraries and the like. The worst thing they can do is allow their minds to become dormant.

Leslie Howie, aged 17, Wallsend, Tyne and Wear

Schools should discuss what it's like to be unemployed, but they don't. They're trying to mould society and they're too scared to explore risky issues. They seem to want a sort of master race in this country as well as average kids who just go out to work, stay at home at weekends and keep the country going smoothly. Instead of going on trips to Stonehenge and places like that, we should go to prisons, dole offices and old people's homes – to see how they cope on their money each week, for instance.

They should teach you more about the problems of sex. When we did about pregnancy it was all on the side of a woman getting married, settling down, having kids and bringing them up, while the man goes to work. I'd say it's up to the girl whether she wants the baby or not; it's not necessarily the man who has to go out to work — it could be the girl.

When you're in school, it's a protected world. I would have learnt faster if I'd knocked off school. I met this kid the other day who stayed on to the sixth form and he said, 'Oh, I don't really believe there are race riots,' and he was going on that down St Pauls they aren't that oppressed. He was saying the police ain't that bad, but that's 'cos he's at school. When you're on the dole, just walking round at night, and you get stopped by the police and arrested 'cos you ain't got enough money or something, you start realising what the world's like, as opposed to sitting in your sixth-form common rooms talking about Led Zepellin and physics and all that crap.

Ray Scanlon, aged 17, Lawrence Weston, Bristol

If they taught stuff in schools like on the life and social skills course at YOP that would be really good, because it'd help you more for life after school. OK some people have their Mum looking after them, but when you leave school you may be on your own and you have to do things like live and cope with situations like signing on, finding work, opening bank accounts, taking a driving test and getting yourself around. The kind of stuff we did in geography about glaciers and ice-ages is terrific if you're going to go into something that involves that. We had one lesson a week on moral and social education, which was supposed to teach the sort of things we now do on life and social skills — but we just concentrated on different religions around the world.

Maxine Irving, aged 19, Camelford, Cornwall

What does education do for someone? What does English actually do? What it *should* do is teach you to think and to ask questions. Say you've got a problem with sex, and someone gives you a book about this kid who's got a problem with his girl friend. It's not you, but as you read it, you begin to ask yourself if you've got the same problem. Books should be about trying to get you to think and question things.

'Tory Crimes', aged 18, Glasgow

'Schools should be about life'

If I ran a school I'd let people know that reading and writing isn't the most important thing. I'd make sure they were taught about the world outside. For instance you don't learn anything about mentally or phys-

35

ically handicapped people, so you see them as something apart from you. If you could see and understand what they're like you'd understand more about yourself. If you could go in as a helper — not taken in so that you just stare at them — but to work with them, help them, talk to them, you'd see them very differently.

Mandy Smith, aged 19, Withywood, Bristol

Our RE teacher was broad-minded and you could talk to him as a friend. We talked about marriage, divorce and other social things. I'd always wanted to be a teacher ever since I was small and as I got older it was RE I wanted to teach.

Catherine Crowe, aged 17, Wardley, West Midlands

School should be about life, but it isnae: it's about separating people out and dividing them up intae categories, by saying you're going intae this class, you're going intae that class; this class will be the people who go tae university, this class will be the people who work in banks, and these people will work in the factories. It should be a preparation for after school instead of being about getting qualified.

Teachers — particularly the older ones — were always saying, 'You'll nae get a job if you didnae work at this.' But they're changing their attitudes slowly and starting tae admit that even if you have a university degree you may possibly nae get a job. Now they have tae say things like, 'You may nae find a job when you leave school, even though you've got all these qualifications, but we think you should do it for yourself, just to prove you can.'

My younger sister who's thirteen came home last week and said her teacher had asked her what a YOP scheme was, and for the first time they discussed employment and unemployment in the class. When I was there and about tae leave the only real discussions were about which university or college you'd apply for and what exams you'd need. Before the exams all they talk about is exams, exams, exams. But exams don't say anything about you as a person. If you're nae going on tae university I dinae see that much point, because for most jobs you didnae actually use your certificates.

I didnae think you need as many certificates as people are trying tae drum into you. A lot of the time it isnae education; you're nae learning anything — just sitting there being disciplined. Education is more than just being lectured at in school.

Mary Seath, aged 17, Edinburgh

Most of what they teach you is a lot of waffle that you never use again. I can understand the reasons for teaching you a cross section of work, but not the sort of stuff they were teaching us. I reckon most of the lessons went on price – the cheapest way to fill our time.

Schools just get the more academic kids ready. They should teach more do-it-yourself skills. Most people don't even know how to hang a piece of wallpaper, yet it's something they'll probably be doing all their lives. Or you could get a couple of old cars in and take them apart. You learn a hell of a lot by taking things to bits. Then you could bring in a scrap merchant to take it all away again. They'd do it for the price of the metal.

Schools shouldn't just concentrate on the ones who are good at the theory side of things. They should also concentrate on the practical side. Somewhere down the line someone's got to decide who's going to be white-collar and who's not – and teach one theory and the other practical.

Phil Bird, aged 21, Hartcliffe, Bristol

I thought gardening was a waste of time. All we done was dig up a patch of earth and put in a few peas. Religious Education used to get right on my nerves. People who like that should go to Sunday school or chapel. This old bloke was babbling on about Jesus, and old Moses and someone turned into salt! God, I used to hate it.

Lynne Wooders, aged 17, St Austell, Cornwall

The trouble was that you'd choose a subject like gardening, but they couldn't supply all the tools because there were too many of us. We were just sitting in the classroom writing about it. You don't learn by doing that. Gardening is planting and digging. Then there was English, and that was just writing from the board. You need to learn some from the past and some from the future, so you know where you stand – a bit like history.

John Masefield, aged 19, Kingstanding, Birmingham

Politics ought to be one of the most important subjects. You come out into the world at sixteen or eighteen, and you know nothing about one of the most important things in your life; so you end up voting for people you don't understand. A party can say we're going to do this, we're going to do that, and you need to be able to see whether it's possible, or whether they're just talking crap. If you're naive enough to know nothing about politics you might vote in someone who's going to knock £30 off your wages in real terms. Politics should be a major subject.

'Tory Crimes', aged 18, Glasgow

Schools ought to open people's eyes to things like violence and things that are illegal; they shouldn't just be blocked out, they ought to be

37

brought into the open, so that people know about them. It shouldn't be simply, 'This doesn't matter — we don't want to talk about that.' Teach them about life. For instance, if some boy's got a problem you can explain the way *you* feel about it, show *your* side of it, and maybe then, somebody who's quite young will see things differently and understand more.

If you need people and they need you, you don't talk about the weather, you start to talk about yourself and your feelings, and their feelings and their view on things. It's really important that people start off on the right foot so that they can leave school with a feeling that they've learnt something, not a feeling of relief, 'Oh great, that's finished. No more of that.' It's over ten years, so it ought to be enjoyable. Childhood is quite an important part of your life.

Jo Chadwick, aged 17, Trowbridge, Wilts

'I had to learn by trial and error'

Schools are meant tae prepare you for life, but you're shattered when you come out because you're in this big wide world, where you've no idea what tae do, I didnae even know where the dole queue was. I think teachers do know these things, but they dinae think it's part of their job tae tell us. They think they're there tae teach subjects, not tae tell us about the dole queue and sex education. The only sex education we had was in biology, where we learnt about the parts of the body. They didnae tell us about contraception. All you've got tae rely on are books or friends that already know. I used tae think you only went tae the Brook Clinic if you were pregnant.

Jayne Harper, aged 16, Edinburgh

We had sex education in the third year. One wonderful lesson. It was simply chaotic! The things flying through the air were quite amazing! It was just a joke really. 'What lesson do you get next?' — 'Sex.' — 'Oh, can I come with you?'

Nicola Northway, aged 16, Longbenton, Newcastle-upon-Tyne

They don't teach you what you really want to learn, like about sex. You don't hear anything in school about the problems of promiscuous sex or VD and all that stuff. I had to learn about it on my own: trial and error: hit and miss.

Marcel Rosari, aged 18, St Austell, Cornwall

There isn't enough sex education. They teach you the physical aspects but nothing about the relationship side of it. The trouble is that parents think schools teach everything nowadays, but there aren't many teachers who are prepared tae talk about those sort of things. . . . Of course everyone picks up the bare facts in time, but it's too important an issue tae just leave tae chance.

When we sent out a questionnaire from where I work now asking young people whether their parents had discussed sex with them, the majority said no. Even the ones who said yes felt embarrassed discussing it with their mothers and fathers, so maybe you *do* need someone apart from your parents — someone who you aren't living with — who you can talk tae. I think it would help if some teachers were trained for this — perhaps by an organisation like the Brook Advisory Clinic.

I can talk tae my parents about almost anything, but my parents have never schooled me in sex education. I've got all these folders from the Brook Clinic lying about in my room and twice I've seen my mother reading them. She'll turn round and say, 'You know more about sex education than I do!'

Jacquie Irving, aged 17, Edinburgh

'Business calculation instead of triangles'

I'd change things like maths completely, because x + y = z is fine for people who are going to do chemistry, and who are going to go on and build rockets — but they ought to learn that sort of thing when they *know* they're going to build rockets. When you're in school they should make sure that you know your times table inside out, and percentages, division and multiplication: simple, basic straight maths.

Wanda Raven, aged 17, Kingstanding, Birmingham

I wish I'd tried harder at school, but it doesn't seem like it's going to get you anywhere, even if you have the qualifications on paper. For example, the maths that we did at school hasn't been any use to me at work. They could have taught us more about business calculations instead of triangles.

Heather Crompton, aged 18, Great Barr, Birmingham

I couldn't see the point of some subjects. In physics I learnt about splitting atoms and Newton's Law, but I've never used any of it since leaving school. It's the same in maths. Things like algebra, algorithms and logarithms aren't as useful as basic multiplication. In geography I learnt about how a volcano erupts, which is all right for scientists, but what I *really* wanted to learn about was sex.

Marcel Rosari, aged 18, St Austell, Cornwall

39

Young people's comments

Now I've left school and faced the 'big wide world' I can look back on the subjects I did at school, see how they've helped me, and suggest some changes.

PE: I think us females should be taught more about the most popular games (football and cricket) so we can understand them better when watching TV or reading the paper.

Geography: This was an example of a subject being too scientific. My lessons consisted of things like learning about soil: why Cornwall was marshy and London used to be but isn't now. I would love to know more about the people in different countries.

Maths: So many of the subjects like calculus I will never use again, whereas adding, takeaways, percentages and so on weren't covered often enough.

Cookery: A lot of it was about baking cakes. I never learnt how to cook a proper three-course meal, or cope with a weekly menu. It would have helped to know about the ideal things to eat at break times when you started work (if you ever did) like a round of sarnies, an apple and some crisps; or a flask of soup and a couple of hard-boiled eggs.

Woodwork: I never learnt how to put up a shelf or how to make a small cupboard (perhaps to box in an electric meter). I can remember once being told to make a 'freaky' sculpture to stick a candle in. What use is that to me?

Metalwork: I was shown how to make pendants and a metal coat hanger, but I'd have preferred to learn about nuts and bolts.

English: I think pupils would be just as interested in how books and newspapers are made as in the stories that go into them.

History: I would like to know more about subjects that were a reality for millions of people – like World War II, or why Russia went Communist.

Music: Music lessons *could* open a door to the reality of today's music industry by teaching about synthesisers, recording studios, how a record is put together, as well as the old-fashioned things like classical music and instruments.

Driving: I reckon half the people that left school at the same time as me have a car or are intending to buy one. School could tell you how to go about this as well as the Highway Code, tax and insurance and the basics of driving and car maintenance.

Money: Perhaps pupils should know why they find that their parents cannot afford 'luxury' items – because they've just got the gas bill, the electricity bill and they're still paying for the house. How do you get a mortgage? How do banks work out their interest?

Ley Alberici, aged 17, Great Barr, Birmingham

40

Part 2 – Exams

'Paper qualifications still count for something'

The problem is that schools still need to concentrate on exams, because paper qualifications still count for something. With a lot of jobs, you can say you're qualified, but if you haven't got a bit of paper proving you're qualified you've had it. I had a friend who was three years through a four-year apprenticeship with a garage when he had an argument with the boss who then kicked him out. He tried to find another job but because he hadn't finished his apprenticeshipp no one would take him on. He's as good as a qualified mechanic, he can do the lot, but because he hasn't got it on paper it's no good.

Geoff Clark, aged 18, Bodmin, Cornwall

I hate the idea of exams but that's the only way you can get by. You have to play with the system. You don't have to agree with it, but you have to accept it a bit. If you rebel against it all the time you won't get anywhere, and all you'll do is damage yourself. It won't change *them*.

Jo Chadwick, aged 17, Trowbridge, Wilts

I wasn't brainy enough to take exams. I could hardly read when I was fifteen.

Angela Burstow, aged 17, Callington, Cornwall

Half of us were clever and half of us weren't. At first I wanted to be clever and I used to listen to the teacher; but as time went on I used to sit further towards the back to be with my friends.

Catherine Crowe, aged 17, Wardley, West Midlands

'Why have O levels to watch Jackanory?'

I don't think such a great emphasis should be placed on O and A levels. I think they should be used more as a guide to show that a guy has been through school in that respect, but it's very difficult to change attitudes. There's got to be lawyers and doctors and blokes who work in the mines, and there has to be a distinction between the two.

Matthew Fforde, aged 17, Easton, Bristol

I left without taking any exams. All my pre-exams were so bad that I thought it would have been pretty worthless. My Mother's attitude was that as long as I could read and write it didn't matter. I'm not lacking in common sense just because I don't know when Henry VIII died, but I feel I'm a doughnut because I haven't got any CSEs. My Mum says that when she interviews girls she has a glut of kids with half a dozen O levels. But even though they're well educated they haven't any common sense. Ask them facts and figures and they know it all, but they're right doughnuts behind the bar.

Jemma Littlefair, aged 17, St Werburgh's, Bristol

Exams are all very well if there's work, but if you're going to sit home all day watching *Rainbow* or *Jackanory*, why have O levels? Your knowledge is just going to go from the front of your head. You think, 'Oh, I've got these O levels, I'm bound to get a job', and you'll sit back for a little while and your knowledge is going to go further and further back 'till it comes to a stage when you've forgotten all about it.

Matthew Brown, aged 17, Chelmsford, Essex

I think sixteen is the right age to make people stay on. You don't have to go out and work in the mines at twelve and you don't have to stay on and become super brains if you don't want to. I remember once sitting down with my art teacher and we worked out that if you were the Brain of Britain and you went in for every exam possible and every course possible, then you could stay in the education system and be supported by the tax payer until you're 39. Brilliant! But what good would it be when I came out? I'd be so highly qualified that no one would want to know. There's guys walking around with university degrees who want the job I've got.

Kerry Parkes, aged 21, Great Barr, Birmingham

Teachers keep pushing you to pass exams: they say if you don't get good exam results, you won't make much of a life for yourself. I suppose that's true to a certain extent, but the way it is now there's not much going for anybody even if they do have exams. They're something to fall back on if you fail in your first job, but they don't really count for much. It's your attitude – your character – that counts as much as how good you are at subjects. Trying to be good at a subject which you find difficult deserves just as much a pat on the back as being good at it because you find it easy.

Bruce Jackman, aged 16, St Austell, Cornwall

'She's really clever, but when it comes to exams she goes to pieces'

My whole mind just goes blank when I'm sitting in rows with everyone writing. I don't know what it is but something blows and I cannae think. The atmosphere's so hard. Everyone is working away and you're thinking, 'I wonder if they're getting the right answers?' You're really strug-gling, but in a *class* exam where the teacher's nae really bothered if you're talking, you can think a lot more clearly and I can work out answers quicker.

Jayne Harper, aged 16, Edinburgh

I think assessment over a period of time would have been much fairer than exams but people say it would be difficult to do that. I've got a friend who's really clever. She can apply everything, but when it comes to exams she goes to pieces. She's failed lots of exams because of that. This year I took statistics O level and I could apply everything in les-son time. I thought I'd pass, but I just couldn't do it in the exam. I sat there looking round and doodling. I know it was the wrong attitude but I couldn't help it.

I don't think exams should count for such a lot. I think you need common sense more than anything. I know some really clever people with no common sense at all. One of my friends can't do anything but apply maths rules to everything. That really annoys me that does. She'll probably get a good job, but not actually be able to do it, because she's so stupid at common-sense things.

Janet Gould, aged 17, Bonsall, Derbyshire

With the competitive system in schools you get experts who pick up the subject naturally. You get ones who struggle along and make it there eventually, and you get ones who are so hopeless that they feel inade-quate. I thing that's what produces a lot of screwed-up kids, because they keep trying to prove themselves. It's the same as sex competitive-ness. All the 'real' guys would come in and say, 'Had a great night last night pal – four, five, six times', or whatever; and the ones that didn't, have to lie and think, 'Oh shit, there's something wrong with me, per-haps I'm gay?' If you can't prove yourself within a certain time you start to have a complex.

Exams shouldn't exist. You can work at your own level. If you're interested, you don't need an exam to motivate you.

'Tory Crimes', aged 18, Glasgow

Part 3 – Uniform – the hidden curriculum?

'You get no class distinction'

I didn't see anything wrong with uniform. I preferred to wear it, be-cause you didn't have to think about what to put on each day. But I think teachers should wear uniform as well. Our English teacher used

43

to wear bright green eye shadow, high shoes, split skirts and red nail varnish — and she'd be walking round saying, 'Your shoes are too high — get that nail varnish off.' You can't set an example if you're doing exactly what you're telling kids not to do.

Joanne Clark, aged 17, Chelmsford, Essex

You get no class distinction with uniform. It doesn't matter whether your parents have a good wage or have financial problems: you all wear the same. If your parents aren't working, you're given a grant.

Brian Carr, aged 17, Forest Hill, Newcastle-upon-Tyne

If you all wear uniform there's no bitchiness between girls who wear fashion stuff and girls who wear normal clothes.

Caroline Asquith, aged 16, Easton, Bristol

'It takes away your individuality'

In terms of rules I think anything that endangers people has to be out. If people are allowed to run round the place all the time, since the school is quite a packed area, there'd be accidents. You'd smash into people with trolleys, so safety-wise rules are sensible. But stuff like school dress should be up to the individual. They say you wear school dress because it makes people look the same. They say you can have a poor person in school dress and a rich person in school dress and they won't look different; but they do 'cos the rich person's got much better cloth or whatever it is, and the poor person's got this old blazer handed down from his brother, so it doesn't work that way.

I didn't wear it. If it was a hot day I used to go in my tee-shirt, and they'd say, 'Why aren't you wearing your tie and your shirt?' and I used to say, 'Because it's too hot.' I'd be put on report or detention for that but detentions seemed pretty useless to me. You do the same thing the next day regardless. It didn't achieve anything being shut up in a little classroom with four or five other kids for an hour after school — doing nothing except sitting there. It's no use really because some teacher is going to have to stay as well and I bet he doesn't like it either. We had a teacher who used to come in for a quarter of an hour and say, 'Go off home, 'cos I want to go home myself'!

Geoff Clark, aged 18, Bodmin, Cornwall

I once organised a strike in the school. We had a big meeting in the lecture theatre about school uniform because we weren't allowed tae wear trousers in the winter. Guys could turn up in jeans or leather jackets or anything but lassies had tae wear navy or blue skirts, a blazer and shirt and tie, and grey tights or white socks. So we decided tae go on strike tae have trousers. This lassie who was Head Girl leaked it tae the Headmistress that there was going tae be a strike on Friday and I was called in front of her and a group of teachers, but I told them it was going ahead whether they knew about it or not. They said they'd take the issue tae the School Council and it was agreed that we should be allowed tae wear trousers between October and April but they had tae be black or navy and not cords or jeans.

I didnae agree with uniform because it takes away your individuality. You cannae look how you want tae look. Most pupils turn up in a blue blazer, blue skirt and tie and shirt, but some kids' parents cannae afford tae buy the uniform so they look different from everyone else. There were six of us in our family — six lassies — so it was a whole uniform for each of us and it meant that my parents couldnae afford as many clothes for me tae go out at night. Sometimes I'd turn up in jeans and they used tae call me up before assembly, give me a games kilt tae wear and take away my jeans till the end of the day. Usually the kilts didnae fit or didnae fasten at the waist, because they were forty sizes too big. That was deliberate so as tae embarrass me.

Mary Seath, aged 17, Edinburgh

The uniform was such a sick colour. A horrible yellow blouse, and a royal blue skirt that stuck out at the sides and stretched when you washed it. If you were in your winter uniform and were caught with the sleeves rolled up or button undone you'd have to write lines and stay in. You weren't allowed to wear ear-rings; they were always telling me to pull mine out.

Lynne Wooders, aged 17, St Austell, Cornwall

See pp. 123-8 for the response by John Mann.

Chapter 4

Teachers

'A good teacher is . . .

Teachers should know that they're not going into a job but a way of
life – and they're doing it through their own choice. That's the difference between them and kids. Kids are there because they've got to be;
teachers are there because they want to be. If they appreciate that,
they'll know that they've got to be understanding and be super-
humanly patient.

Kerry Parkes, aged 21, Great Barr, Birmingham

School is about learning and you can't get away from it. But there's
different ways tae teach. Some teachers just put it over really good and
make you learn things without you realising you're learning. We went
tae a dairy culture farm recently, and there was a girl there with young
kids and it was amazing how she kept their attention, and was teaching
them at the same time. She didnae say, 'This is a cow and it has so
many udders,' or, 'This is a milking machine.' She'd say, 'This is a cow,
would you like tae feel it? Come and touch it, this is where the milk
comes from.' The way she kept their attention was brilliant; she was
really good with kids. That's the way you've got tae do it in schools.

Jayne Harper, aged 16, Edinburgh

A good teacher is someone with a lot of patience, who tries to show no
favouritism at all and who is prepared to listen to your point of view.
When you reach fourteen or fifteen you develop your own opinions.
I think the trouble with a lot of teachers is that they aren't prepared
to listen to young people's ideas. If teachers were to hold more discussions in the classroom, rather than tell you points, the teacher-pupil
relationship could improve a great deal.

Helen Ashworth, aged 19, Sutton Coldfield, West Midlands

A good teacher is one with a sense of humour, but who is quite strict so you can't go too far. Some teachers have a way so that they can control the class without having to use the belt. I've had the belt three times. Twice was by a really pathetic Latin teacher who would line six of you up and belt you and it just didn't hurt at all; it was hysterical. The other was by this man for forgetting my jotter three times. He absolutely walloped me, and I didn't like him after that — but he was a good teacher. Being able to control classes is an ability some teachers have and some don't. Some can control the class but are absolutely hopeless teachers. Yet other teachers who can't control the class are really good teachers and the ones who want to learn come round to them.

> Yvonne Gray, aged 19, Marchment, Edinburgh

The best teachers are those who aren't trying to project their authority all the time — who feel secure in allowing you to go so far and no further.

> Nicola Northway, aged 16, Longbenton, Newcastle-upon-Tyne

The worst teachers were the oldest teachers — the ones who said, 'We fought the war for people like you.' If I was there I'd have fought it myself. It wasn't my fault I wasn't born then.

> Mark Baker, aged 19, Bretton, Peterborough

Once, when we went away on a rugby trip to play a team in Beverley, Yorkshire, they took along a teacher we didn't like in school. But we got on well with him at the weekend 'cos he was different. We found that he was human. But he became the same person again when he got back to school. We'd say, 'hello' in the corridor and he'd just reply with, 'Where are *you* going? Get out!' — that sort of thing.

> Andrew Seal, aged 19, Great Barr, Birmingham

'The way teachers start lessons is important'

The best teacher taught us maths for a double period on Monday morning. He'd start off by saying 'Had a nice weekend everyone?' and he'd ask people what they'd done and sometimes we'd all fold up on the floor with laughter. He'd even come out with jokes himself. Then he'd say, 'Let's get on with some work, take your books out' and that was it. We'd all be quiet and get on with our work or we'd sit there and talk to each other and he'd say, 'Could you be quiet, there's a lesson next door.' He was sociable. He just gave out the work and let you get on with it, and said, 'Any trouble — come up and see me.' Some teachers,

47

they walk into the classroom and straight away it's, 'Right, be quiet, sit down, get your books out and shut up.'

The way teachers start lessons is important. If the minute you get in there they shout at you, you think, 'Oh Christ, here we go.' If you go to talk to somebody and it's, 'Oi, shut up!', that's when it all comes out, because it boils up inside you. You think, 'Christ, he ain't going to rule me.'

Matthew Brown, aged 17, Chelmsford, Essex

I'd say that being able to talk with teachers is important but then I'm older now. I don't think I particularly wanted to talk to them when I was younger. Mind you, if you're shy, like I was, you can't talk in a group, so it helps if teachers talk to you individually. The trouble is that teachers need time: when you've got 30 pupils in a class, it's pretty impossible to talk to them individually. I enjoyed the subjects where I liked the teacher — even if I wasn't very good at the subject. I dreaded going to the lessons where I was frightened of the teacher. Of course, teachers shouldn't be so soft that pupils take advantage of them, but I think the majority prefer a relaxed atmosphere.

Janet Gould, aged 17, Bonsall, Derbyshire

To teach you need to make a bond between you and the class. They need to see you as a centre of information, and you have to make them feel they want it and need it. You have to form a trust between a teacher and the class, and you have to treat everyone as an individual. I'm not a number; I'm someone; I'm me. I may not be the greatest thing on earth, but I'm someone with a personality and interests.

'Tory Crimes', aged 18, Glasgow

There were a lot of teachers who said, 'If you've got a problem about anything, you can always come and see me,' which I think is good because it means there's always someone you can talk to if you need to — although I know some people would say, 'I'm not telling *teachers* my problem!'

Kristine King, aged 18, Bretton, Peterborough

They should be interested in what you're doing, but I don't think I'd talk about *very* personal things with a teacher. They can't really appreciate your situation.

Nicola Northway, aged 16, Longbenton, Newcastle-upon-Tyne

'You need to respect teachers'

I knew some teachers well, but a lot seemed quite removed. They'd just work from nine till four and that was it. I suppose it's hard to treat people individually if you're with classes of 30–40 for six hours a day. I think they should try and treat kids more as adults and give them more responsibility, since that's what they need when they leave school. You're really protected when you're at school. Whilst you're there it's just school and home all the time, but when you leave and there's no jobs, you're on your own, except for your parents.

The art teacher seemed to give us that responsibility. Because he had the attitude of being a friend, he got a certain respect. You thought, 'He's letting me do this in my own time, in my own way, so I won't abuse it.' You never used to go slow and he always seemed interested in what you were doing. But then our group was only fifteen in size, which meant he *could* spend more time with each person.

Geoff Clark, aged 18, Bodmin, Cornwall

You build up a great thing that teachers are teachers and they're not people, which is crazy because they *are* people underneath; they're not robots. They're hesitant to become involved with pupils, but I think the only way you can get authority that's going to work is by respect. It's all very well shouting at a kid but whether he's going to listen or not is a different matter. You might shut him up for ten minutes but you don't know if he's going to take note of what you're saying.

The problem is the size of the classes. Thirty kids is crazy. Groups ought to be about fifteen in size. You could do it by bringing in people who weren't teachers. That way schools could teach you home maintenance like what to do if the telly blows up or the tap leaks. You could teach about car mechanics and re-spraying in small groups. You could do craft work at an individual level. All it would need is people who know what they're talking about; they don't need to have passed exams!

Jo Chadwick, aged 17, Trowbridge, Wilts

I think they should be strict, but not so that you're scared of them. I've enjoyed most of my lessons where I've had a strict teacher who's been friendly. It's a difficult balance, which the older teachers are better at achieving because they've had experience at handling kids. Student teachers were hopeless because they tried to be friendly thinking that if the class liked them, they'd do as they're told. We used to have one boy who'd do the same trick every time. He'd drop his pencil and then go on about not being able to do his work and the teacher would give him a pencil while his own pencil was on the floor. Then he'd start humming the bread advert, just to see how far he could push the teacher. It's a sort of game — testing out new teachers. Kids in school are quite cruel to teachers, but if everyone else is doing it you can't turn round and say, 'No, I'm not going to join in.' You'd get pretty funny treatment then.

Teachers are a fair lot on the whole, but although they're trying to prepare you for leaving school and getting a job, they don't really trust you; they won't leave doors unlocked, for instance. It's partly because one minute they're teaching a group of twelve-year-olds who they have to treat in one way and the next minute they're teaching a group of seventeen-year-olds. Half way through the lesson they'll begin to treat you like you're meant to be, but by then they've probably put their oar in already.

> Cheryl Davidson, aged 17, Bretton, Peterborough

It would make me feel uncomfortable if I called teachers by their Christian names in school. It wouldn't feel right.

> Tracy Atkinson, aged 16, Longbenton, Newcastle-upon-Tyne

I'd be walking down the corridor and one of the teachers would say, 'Hey, Masefield!' Well, that's no way to treat you is it? It ain't as if they don't know your name, 'cos you've been there long enough. I mean five years is a long time. There's no reason why they should call you by your surname. I think that provokes a lot of kids at school.

> John Masefield, aged 19, Kingstanding, Birmingham

In multi-racial education the teacher was very pro-black. He was almost prejudiced against white people. He stuck up so much for the black people. I thought he was great for them, but they didn't like him. They used to hate multi-racial education. He'd ask a question and all the white kids would put their hands up, but he wouldn't let them answer. He was always going for the black kids and he used to drive the white people mad, but the coloured kids didn't seem to have any respect for him 'cos he had no respect for white people. Some teachers, like the one in multi-racial education, try to get round the kids by being one of the kids, laughing and joking, but that way you lose their respect and you can't tell them to shut up or anything because you've become one of them. I respected the strict teachers

> Jemma Littlefair, aged 17, St Werburgh's, Bristol

My school was all girls before it went comprehensive. When I first went in it was quite amusing because although the first, second and third years were comprehensive and mixed, the fourth, fifth and sixth years were elegant young ladies. Certain teachers that you knew would be going out with the girls in the sixth year, which is one of the reasons I wouldn't go away with the school on camps. Because they didn't have any boys in their classes, the sixth-form girls were absolutely men daft. We used to talk about it in the common room — about what married teacher went out with which girl. I don't think the teachers were really taking it seriously but I think they should have been more responsible and not taken advantage of girls' vulnerability. It made it hard to respect them.

Yvonne Gray, aged 19, Marchmont, Edinburgh

'He seemed to care about the kids'

In the fifth year we had a bloke who actually seemed to care more about the kids he was teaching than doing his job. He used to take us out when it was really boiling hot and sweaty in the classroom, and there was one time when he bought a tub of ice cream and we all had ice cream. No one in the class disliked him. He just seemed to care more about the kids.

Andy James, aged 20, Lawrence Weston, Bristol

A lot of teachers believe that everything they tell you is gospel, but we had a good English teacher who'd listen to us. We'd go miles off the subject but we'd listen to his points, and he'd listen to our points and we'd usually come to some sort of compromise. It wasn't just somebody standing at the front saying, 'I'm right — you listen.'

Wanda Raven, aged 17, Kingstanding, Birmingham

If a teacher takes more interest in the backward kids, and at some time during the day spends ten or fifteen minutes just talking to them and sort of relates to them as a friend, then maybe you could encourage backward kids to do more reading and writing. He could explain that if you can't read and write very well then your choice of jobs is going to be very limited. If you talk to a kid like that as a friend it's easier to relate and then you can ask if he wants any help. If a teacher won't waste any time on you, then what? A pupil isn't geared to think, 'I'm not doing very well in class — I must go and get help', because when you're young you don't like to admit you need help for reading and writing — or anything else for that matter. It's difficult to admit you need help.

Gordon MacMillan, aged 23, Baptist Mills, Bristol

Young people's comments

'If you like a teacher you like the lesson'

With the games teacher we could talk about anything: about what you'd done the night before and all that. Me and my mate had given up smoking and we found out that the games teacher had given up smoking as well, so we had a kind of competition between us. You couldn't have done that with any other teachers; they would have reported you to the Head for smoking. I was in teams for most things at school which is probably why I liked the games teacher. I'd see her a lot after school and on Saturdays. I don't see her now but I did when I was at school. I don't want to see any of the teachers now. I'm glad to be rid of that school. It got me my qualifications but I don't think it did owt else for me.

Deb Cannon, aged 18, Lancaster

I got on with metalwork, woodwork, technical drawing and general studies teachers. You could approach them in a different way than the others. When you were stuck you could put your hand up and they'd say, 'OK,' and they'd come and help. But with the others when you were sitting in the classroom and you put your hand up, they'd just say, 'Hang on a minute.' But they were doing nothing really, just sitting behind the desk, and it was too much trouble to walk to you.

John Masefield, aged 19, Kingstanding, Birmingham

If you like a subject and they know you're showing an interest they try to help a lot more. But I think they should also give attention to those that don't like it and help them round it. I find students a lot friendlier than some teachers because they're sort of new to the subject, and if you're new at the school they're just the same as you really.

Trish Doherty, aged 17, Lancaster

In metalwork they always used to come round to see if you were stuck or owt, whereas in maths if you couldn't get on with it they just left you alone. I *wanted* to do some of my subjects, but if I was a bit stuck or slow the teacher would hardly ever come and explain it properly. They always seemed to spend time with the ones who could do it. I suppose they thought I wasn't worth bothering with because I mucked about. But if they'd helped me I'd have got on much better with them. In rural science, for example, which I really wanted to do, they always used to send me and my mate Martin up to town to get sawdust for the rabbits, or up to the top field to feed the hens. I didn't say owt because I knew they'd take no notice of me.

Colin Ryder, aged 19, Bonsall, Derbyshire

Teachers are human aren't they? So are the kids. So why don't they treat them as if they were *their* children? Why don't they explain things? They could say 'If you revise you *might* get an exam at the end and it *might* help you get a job,' rather than 'You've *got* to do it.' The best teachers are those you can talk to and create a good atmosphere.

Ley Alberici, aged 17, Great Barr, Birmingham

Teachers have to find a way to make it enjoyable for you to want to come to school. If you like a teacher, you like going to his lesson and you learn more than you would with a very strict teacher.

Brian Carr, aged 17, Forest Hill, Newcastle-upon-Tyne

There was one young part-time teacher who was there instead of somebody else, and he was great. He was only about twenty-two and he was just like us; he told jokes. When we was out in the field he'd give us a fag to smoke in the corner and things like that — he was all right. He was soft in one way but strict in another. He let you do things, but if you messed him about you'd regret it more. He wouldn't send you to the Head. He'd just outcast you from the class and that'd make you feel worse because you wanted to get on with him. He took me for technical drawing as well. I couldn't do technical drawing in the slightest before he come, but he was always with the people who couldn't do it right. To the ones who shouted, 'I've finished, Sir, I've finished, Sir' he would say, 'All right you've finished — put it in your folder — I'll look at it after.' He'd come round and he'd show you how to do it, and he'd do it for you and tell you to do it again. He learnt me how to do technical drawing — he learnt me how to do all sorts.

Brian McMenamin, aged 17, Lancaster

'Some teachers thrive by embarrassing you'

Some teachers thrive by embarrassing you and showing you up, like when you have to wear skirts up to your thighs during games and you don't want to — partly because the boys are out playing soccer. They'd say, 'Take it up' and I would, but it's ever so degrading. I know it's easier to run, but with skirts up to there and the wind blowing you feel terrible. It makes you feel really little again.

Mandy Smith, aged 19, Withywood, Bristol

In comprehensive school there's a tremendous distance between you and the teachers. I had to keep reminding myself that they did have a life outside; that they had a family and kids of their own. When you're in a classroom it's a very closed-up thing. If a teacher tells you something it kind of blocks out everything else. He's a teacher, nothing else, and that's how you judge what he's putting across to you. The only teacher I really loathed was the games master. I was just so incompetent at any kind of sport, and he'd belittle me for not doing something right. He'd pull me out of the crowd and make me show them I wasn't any good.

To keep discipline you need to command respect and that's a natural thing; you can't teach it to anybody. Since the atmosphere in a school depends on the personality of the teachers, you need to try and select those who command respect.

Barrie McGovern, aged 21, Bodmin, Cornwall

We had situations where teachers always had their class pets: children who they adored and thought were great workers, just because they were smartly dressed and said, 'Yes Sir, no Sir.' The teachers used to say they were ideal pupils, while the rest of us were shoved to one side. That seemed unfair when you're all trying.

Ley Alberici, aged 17, Great Barr, Birmingham

We had one really tough guy who was a hopeless speller. The teacher made him stand up and spell 'adventurous' when he was still at the cat and dog stage. He couldn't do it, and the teacher was going, 'What's wrong with you, are you a thick shit? Are you dumb?' One day the same guy had done something wrong and the teacher called him out in front of the class and gave him ten or twelve belts. He made sure this guy had tears in his eyes. To cry in front of all those people was the biggest embarrassment of that guy's life. I'm surprised that teacher walked out alive.

'Tory Crimes', aged 18, Glasgow

'I used to be terrified of some teachers'

They made you more scared than anything. The kids used to think, 'Any minute now the ruler's going to go across my knuckles,' and then you don't take *anything* in. Instead of making kids shit themselves they should be more like parents. I'd love to ask teachers how the hell they think they can help kids if they slag them down so much. It's easy to make other kids laugh if you tell someone off, but it's really unfair.

Lise Palme, aged 21, Bodmin, Cornwall

I used to be terrified of some teachers but you have to reach a point where you just don't let them worry you. At primary school Mrs Macleod used to yell and yell at me in front of the whole class and I

developed a technique of switching off. It's been very helpful since, so
that now, in shorthand, which I'm not particularly good at and where
the teacher is always over my desk and going on at me, I know I'm not
going to give up. I just think, 'So, she's going to yell at me, so what?'
It doesn't frighten me. I think having Mrs Macleod has innoculated me
against being terrified of teachers.

Yvonne Gray, aged 19, Marchmont, Edinburgh

'What matters is self-discipline'

If you messed around you were sent to the Headmaster or the Deputy
Head. The Head weren't bad, but his Deputy used to shout at you and I
were frightened of him. He was rough and used to knock you around.
Once when I was running through the hall, which you weren't supposed
to do in case you tripped someone up and hurt 'em, he grabbed me,
played hell with me and hit me. I walked out of the door and went
home. He sent letters to my parents, but I used to get there before me
Mum and throw 'em away. But when my Dad went up to a school
parents' evening, he came back and told me to get me finger out.

Colin Ryder, aged 19, Bonsall, Derbyshire

They need to be able to listen to your point of view, so that even if it's
wrong they'd listen first before shutting you up. Some teachers would
just say, 'Wrong,' and butt in. I remember once there was this lad who
was a bit of a mouther, yapping away all the time. The teacher grabbed
him by the throat and started throttling him and shaking him about. I
suppose he deserved something, but not that much. It soon shut him up
though. I liked most of my teachers, especially the women, but you
didn't seem to be able to get near them. They didn't want to listen half
the time! It's, 'Go away, I'm busy,' if you try and tell 'em something.
If it's the other way round and you're not listening to *them* in class,
it's whack – a bit of chalk round the lug!

Alan Myerscough, aged 20, Lancaster

We had a PE teacher who was also a part-time copper and a magistrate.
He was orientated towards discipline and his fun used to be a game called
'Hare and Hounds', where you had to chase someone around with a
slipper. If you caught them you smacked them across the arse. He also
liked a game called 'Murder Ball'. There were goal posts about sixteen
to twenty foot wide. He stood in the middle with the ball, chucked it
up, moved out of the way and everyone else made a scrum for the ball.
You weren't allowed to bite, that was the only rule. You had to get the
ball between the posts. You could kick it, kick people, punch people,

but you weren't allowed to bite. I think he was just sadistic!

Geoff Clark, aged 18, Bodmin, Cornwall

My favourite teacher was Mr McIntosh who taught us physics. He did nae treat you quite so childishly. He didnae belt you and he didnae hand out lines just because you hadnae done your homework. He would listen tae your answer for it, and then he'd tell you tae do it, and explain if you didnae do it it was your own fault. That's different tae saying, 'You must do it, or you'll get three of the belt.'

We could call him Tosh and he didnae mind and I didnae lose any respect for him. I really don't see why teachers and pupils can't be on first name terms. Tosh did a lot of things that other teachers didnae. We could go and sit on his desk and talk tae him or he would come and sit on our desks. We used tae sit in a circle so that everyone could talk across the classroom, rather than sitting in rows facing the teacher.

When people say you need more discipline in schools they mean more rules and strict teachers, but that's missing the point because when pupils leave school they don't have people disciplining them. What matters is self-discipline. You can't teach it − it's something people develop for themselves but you have tae give people the opportunity so that they can learn what's right and wrong by making decisions for themselves. If they work, they'll do well; if they didnae, then that's their fault and you have to allow them tae fail. The way teachers talk tae pupils is important. If a teacher talks *at* you, you didnae really listen, but if you're discussing something on the same sort of level *with* a teacher, you learn much more. If you say tae pupils 'Sit there and read this,' and don't allow them a chance tae voice their opinion, you'll have less control than if you'd involved them in making the decision about what tae read. I think more than anything else pupils need tae be involved in school, otherwise they're just shut out and they're only there tae be taught. You have tae encourage pupils tae actually *take part* in lessons.

Mary Seath, aged 17, Edinburgh

'Once teachers have got something against you that's it'

Teachers didn't get me involved. People expected me to be like my brothers who'd been there before me. The first comment I got was, 'Oh, no, not another Bird.' It made me feel really out of it and because that's what they expected, that's what I was like. I gave up too easily at school. Teachers ought to try and find out where kids get their anti-school attitudes from.

Phil Bird, aged 21, Hartcliffe, Bristol

In cookery class I really worked on my pre-exam practical, doing a five-course meal. I came in early, got all my plates laid out, washed my glasses, spread my tablecloth, put on my apron and worked really hard for a neat presentation. Then one of the teachers came in and said something critical, and I thought, well if you can do a better job, you'd better bloody well do it. He was picking on the way I'd laid out my plates, so I told him what I thought, and I was marched straight to the Headmistress. She said, 'I won't have you being rude to teachers,' and I said, 'I won't have teachers criticising me when I've worked really hard.' So she said, 'Well, I don't know what to do to you for punishment,' and I said, 'I don't bloody well care.' Then she gave me some lines and whacked me on the hand with a ruler, and I was so mad I stormed out. When a prefect said to me, 'What's the matter with you?' I was so angry that I hit him, and I got into trouble again for that.

> Carole Conway, aged 17, St Austell, Cornwall

Some teachers treat you as an animal, as if you're all hooligans. They don't give you a chance. If you're in a class that's got a bad reputation, even if you sit and work, they still don't want to know half the time. When I came back after I'd had the baby, I really wanted to work, but everyone was messing around. Every time I put my hand up, the teacher would be telling someone off, so he didn't take any notice of me. I think they should just leave the people who *don't* want to work and concentrate on helping the people who *do* want to.

> Ronny Moore, aged 17, Southminster, Essex

If they were organising a school trip, and I put my name down, they'd say, 'No,' to me straight away. They never gave me a chance because they didn't trust me to behave. But you see in this children's home they do give you a chance and they do trust you. When I first came here I used to tell lies, do anything to get out of things, but now I don't dare tell a lie because they trust us. You can go out with £40 and spend it on clothes as long as you bring the receipts back. I'd not done that before. It makes you want to not do things because they trust you. I don't tell lies anymore. I guess I just really trust *them*.

> Denise Hegyesi, aged 16, Whitley Bay, Northumberland

Once teachers have got something against you, that's it. You haven't a chance. If there's a lad who does something wrong but then goes straight, they'll always hold the grudge against him. If anything goes wrong they'll always turn to him and say, 'I bet it was you.'

> Dylan Williams, aged 17, Newquay, Cornwall

'You don't think of them as people'

You don't think of them as people. It sounds hard to believe — kids thinking that teachers aren't people — but that's how it is. If you saw them down town or something you couldn't believe it. You used to say 'Oh look, Mrs So and So' and stand there amazed, especially if they'd said 'Hello' to you. But you never thought of them as real people! If a teacher could show that he's a real person, by saying something about himself, perhaps it wouldn't be such a battle in school with teachers on one side and kids on the other. You never see them as doing a job that they enjoy.

You should be able to see them as people with other lives, like they're married, so they know what marriage is about and they form relationships with people. I know it sounds crude, but you never think of them sleeping with anybody. You never think of them going down the pub and drinking beer. They never catch buses; you don't think they've lived and got real knowledge.

Mandy Smith, aged 19, Withywood, Bristol

It's important for teachers to listen and not just play the teacher role. Our maths teacher was a good teacher. If you had a problem or anything like that, she would sit down and talk to you, and if it was real bad, she would say, 'Don't bother working today; just leave it until tomorrow, you might feel better.' But she had to leave 'cos she got pregnant. The trouble is that in school time they've got to say 'Do this and do that,' and they've got to be like monsters and not like human beings. Out of school the teachers always seemed to be more understanding and they would stop and have a laugh with you. I was involved in one of the biggest school plays ever done in Cornwall, where we transformed the whole of the hall into a big castle. I used to stay behind to help. There was always teachers there as well and we used to buy chips together for tea. I'd do the car park and we used to get a cup of coffee afterwards. They treat you differently out of school and it makes you want to work harder when you're with them in school.

Mike Escott, aged 17, Newquay, Cornwall

If you've got kids messing about, teachers always see it as being naughty and tell them to shut up, but there's usually a reason. They're probably very bored or just not interested in what's going on, so shouting at them isn't going to make them stop. Teachers ought to say, 'Why don't you want to do maths?' and try to understand your feelings, rather than just take the attitude that you're at school so you've got to do this. I liked the art teacher, because she treated me as a person. If I was drawing a picture she would say, 'I can see the idea behind that,'

and that would lead on to something else. I did one of a wall with
CND written on it, like it had been spray painted, and she said, 'Why
don't you think there should be nuclear weapons in this country?' I
could see her as a person, not just as a teacher.

Jo Chadwick, aged 17, Trowbridge, Wilts

The system of Sir and Miss is all wrong. If you call them Sir and Miss
you don't realise that when they go home they live normal lives. To me
the teachers were like robots.

Kevin Davis, aged 18, St George, Bristol

'Teacher training should be altered more than the teaching of kids'

To become a teacher students should have to spend more time in
schools than just a month or two. They should learn along with the
kids, and go around asking the kids what they really think and feel.
At the end of their four years they should have tests on how well they
can teach a class. They should be given a week to teach the class something, and then the *kids* should be asked how they got on with that
teacher. At the moment students just have a written test which is
probably going to allow them to affect a million kids in their life time.

Ray Scanlon, aged 17, Lawrence Weston, Bristol

Teachers need to learn psychology, learn about the mind and how to
motivate it, so that they create a sort of lust for knowledge in the classroom. They're not just there to teach straight subjects; they're there to
teach social skills as well. If you teach a subject by making children
memorize facts, like in history, you might as well be a tape recorder.
The crucial thing is being able to motivate children and children need
to be ready for that. Should education start at five or sixteen? In my
case, it's sixteen, because I'm a helluva lot easier to motivate now. I'm
lusting for knowledge, whereas at five I couldn't give a shit.

'Tory Crimes', aged 18, Glasgow

I'd make teachers pass a second certificate at thirty-five and another
at fifty – just to keep them up with the ideas of today. In fifteen years
a lot can change.

Leslie Howie, aged 17, Wallsend, Tyne and Wear

Obviously they could do a lot more, but you're talking about human
beings. Teachers are human beings and unless they're taught to teach
people and taught to understand better then the system will stay the
same. To start that off during teacher training would be a great help.

59

Young people's comments

Teacher training should be altered more than the teaching of kids. If a
young person goes to teacher training college and gets taught the wrong
way, then they're going to teach kids the wrong way.

I think they should be encouraged to find out *why* certain kids are
troublesome at school. Why do they create hell in class? Is it because
they need attention? Why do some kids knock off from school? What
do they get away from school that they don't get at school? What
classes would they prefer? No kid thinks that *everything* in school is
boring.

Gordon MacMillan, aged 23, Baptist Mills, Bristol

A good teacher is somebody who actually wants tae be a teacher and
can relate tae pupils. You get all sorts of pupils: rebellious pupils, quiet
ones, ones that fit in the system brilliant, and you need somebody who
can really relate tae every type. Maybe it's a failing in the colleges
because they only prepare them tae teach subjects. The games teachers
were the worst. I think they had an inferiority complex because they
had a diploma and not a degree and they were always trying tae prove
themselves tae other teachers.

Maureen McLaughlin, aged 18, Edinburgh

'Teachers need a lot of patience'

There were a couple of comics in our class who were always making
noises and things like that, which they thought was really funny, but I
found it quite childish really. The teacher would move them round in
the class. One of them, was a right case; it was incredible the way he
acted. He'd sit there giggling all lesson. My form teacher spent hours
trying to make him feel like an adult and trying to get him to grow up
a little bit. It was hard for the teachers having to spend time with him
when they could have been teaching the rest of the class. It would've
been quite fair if they'd said, 'Sod you,' to him. But they didn't.

Bruce Jackman, aged 16, St Austell, Cornwall

I wouldn't say that it's only in the C form that kids are rowdy. When I
was in the A stream we had some right loonies. It was more like *Not the
Nine O'clock News*, or *Monty Python*. Teachers need to be able to
handle that whether it's in the A form or the C form. The only difference is that with C forms a teacher probably needs to be stricter. Whatever the classes though, they should be able to communicate with all
pupils and create an atmosphere of trust.

Leslie Howie, aged 17, Wallsend, Tyne and Wear

60

A teacher should be able to take a lot of abuse and not to see it as a personal grudge. It's just kids trying to show off.

'Tory Crimes', aged 18, Glasgow

Perhaps a lot of pupils con teachers as well, like saying, 'I don't care.' And they wind them up by whistling and spitting at people or throwing pencils. They do it for show. How do you break that down?

Kerry Parkes, aged 21, Great Barr, Birmingham

Teachers need a lot of patience. There's usually boys at the back who muck around and you've got to try not to lose your temper. Teachers need friendship with their pupils, but kids need to give them a chance and quieten down a bit first so the teachers can respond. It's a teacher's personality that matters really.

Andrew Constance, aged 18, Wadebridge, Cornwall

See pp. 129-33 for the response by John Eggleston.

Chapter 5

Schooled to work

Part 1 – Careers guidance

'If it's like this when I leave school, I should be OK'

A friend from another school did some work experience in his last
year and I thought that would have helped me a lot. From school life
to working life is a big step. They could have broken you in gradually.
Going to work scares you. Half past eight to five, working non-stop, is
very different from nine to four, sitting down writing all day.

Robert Morris, aged 17, Sutton Coldfield, West Midlands

The last six months at school we had half an hour a week with teachers
trying to tell us how to go about an interview, how to write letters for
jobs, and what to do if you wanted to go to college. The teachers
seemed interested. If you knew what you wanted to do they'd talk
about it. I was keen on window designing and the school arranged six
weeks for me on day release, which was quite good really. Some pupils
doing day release managed to get jobs out of it, but I didn't. It was
all right though, because you were getting a grab of what work was
really like and you thought, 'If it's like this when I leave school, I
should be OK.'
    The only trouble with the school was that they were always going
on about how to get a job, but they never mentioned anything about
unemployment. They never told you anything about going on the dole,
social security, and things like that. It was all, 'When you go for a
job . . .' or 'When you get a job.'

Ley Alberici, aged 17, Great Barr, Birmingham

If they treat you like a child or adolescent until you leave school, then
you aren't prepared for adult life. At our school though I found that if

you acted responsibly they'd give you responsibility. The Deputy Head, for instance, used to help me — not by saying, 'You've got to do so and so,' but by saying, 'What do *you* think you should do?' and discussing it with me.

Bruce Jackman, aged 16, St Austell, Cornwall

In the really good lessons they taught you how to look for a job and what to say to an employer. In consumer education you had to go out and buy a week's shopping and learn about how to live in your own home and how to look after it. You wouldn't have done that in a mixed school, because they thought boys wouldn't want to know that. But you need to be taught what life is like when you leave school. Some kids just don't have a clue about what to do.

Caroline Asquith, aged 16, Easton, Bristol

'Careers are middle-class; jobs are working-class'

Yes, it all depends on how you act in your interview whether or not you find out anything useful. In the fourth year I was interested in everything, but by the fifth year it was just the police force, and the careers teacher was trying to persuade me to join the air force or the navy. 'Here you are, pet, have this.' She left me with an envelope, but it had nothing about the police force.

Deborah Barton, aged 16, Longbenton, Newcastle-upon-Tyne

They took the clever ones away for lectures about prospectuses for university, and I was put in tae that but they knew fine well I didnae want tae go. The only other one we had was about the army and the police and I didnae want tae join either of them.

Maureen McLaughlin, aged 18, Edinburgh

I thought that when I left school I'd go on the dole or to the mushroom farm. They used to ask us to write down what job we'd want to do and I'd say, 'Writer or working in a stable,' but I knew I'd never be able to do that. It was just a dream, so I never took any notice of careers lessons.

Mandy Smith, aged 19, Withywood, Bristol

Most of the careers teaching was about the navy, the forces and specific jobs like engineering. There *are* other jobs, aren't there? We didn't have a chance to do work experience, but I went to college one morning a week to do motor vehicle maintenance, but it was a lot of theory. It would have helped if they'd shown us how to look for jobs, not just in

63

Job Centres. If you only go to the Job Centre once a week that won't get you nowt, because the perfect job could have been there the day before. You have to go round firms and ask, because if you just write off, they don't often reply, and if they do it's always, 'Position filled.'

Alan Myerscough, aged 20, Lancaster

In your last year they give you careers lessons and you do things like practising filling in your name on forms, and they tell you about various jobs, but it's more in line for people who want a career. Most of the kids that I knew in my school weren't going into bank work or anything like that. When you go for my sort of job there aren't forms or applications; it's just an interview. Most of us were told we could go and work down the docks or somewhere like that — sort of dead-end jobs. I didn't want that, but I didn't want a career either.

A career is something that's going to last you your whole life time; you start off at the bottom and try and work your way up; the pay gets better, conditions, everything. But a job is something you start and you don't progress much, and it's really boring: you just do it and you stay in a rut all your life. If you're a lawyer or something, that's a career. Careers have status. If you have a career you're middle-class; if you've got a job, you're working-class. My Dad's a bricklayer, so I'm working-class.

Ray Scanlon, aged 17, Lawrence Weston, Bristol

I was looking forward to leaving school, but it's different when you've been out for a couple of months. After a year I was chatting to people and I said I wouldn't mind going back again. You come out with all these big plans and it all starts going wrong.

Andy James, aged 20, Lawrence Weston, Bristol

The programme of the school was to produce robots for industry. I was programmed to think that I wanted to leave and find a job and earn a lot of money and get myself pissed as a newt for six days of the week — or seven. I seriously wanted to do that. I didn't go to see the careers officer. 'Careers officer? Piss off, we're playing cards!'

Working-class people are directed towards the factories by schools and the middle class are directed towards university. Even at thirteen or fourteen you could tell which kids were earmarked for that, and we never ever mixed with them.

'Tory Crimes', aged 18, Glasgow

'If you have fifty interviews, you might still be unemployed'

The English teacher tried to drum it into us about going for interviews dressed smart. 'Make sure your hair's combed and you're nice and clean, and call him Sir.' In other words creep like hell until you've got the job. But I think people should be taken for how they are, then you know if they're worthy of a job or not. People say how you dress is what you are, so that if you have clean boots you're a nice person; it's a load of bull.

School doesn't prepare kids for the outside world, so when they leave it's something of a shock. Maybe schools should take them out and show them what life really is like outside. *Nationwide* did a programme about living like a dosser in London. It showed you what could become of you if you didn't get off your arse and find something for yourself. Schools don't show you the really nasty side of life.

Marcel Rosari, aged 18, St Austell, Cornwall

It would have helped if they'd explained that even if you have fifty interviews you might still be unemployed. I always wanted to be a motor mechanic and I had a chance of a job with Bidwells in Gloucester Road. But the old man explained to me that the day of the motor mechanic would soon be over – that they were ten a penny nowadays and that my best bet would be to become a panel beater. At that time I was blind to the fact that to have only one goal – to be a motor mechanic and nothing else – would be my downfall. I never did find a mechanic's job. Had it been explained to me at school as well – that no matter what you want as a job you might have to compromise – then maybe I'd have taken the panel-beating job.

Gordon MacMillan, aged 23, Baptist Mills, Bristol

I did want a job. I tried. I wrote hundreds of letters and had half a dozen interviews. I'd dress up and comb my hair but they just said, 'Sorry, you're not shortlisted.' I knew when I left school there wouldn't be much chance of getting a job. Careers spend months and months talking about jobs – what you can do, what happens if you're injured at work and so on – but you have to get a fucking job first!.

I thought there'd not be much chance of finding a job, knowing me and my attitude. I'm not as clever as other people. They'll choose people with hundreds of O levels and things. But there's a difference between being intelligent and being bright. Bright is knowing what's going on, and looking after yourself; intelligence is just someone knowing books. They don't teach you how to be bright at school; they teach you to be intelligent.

Tony Hunt, aged 17, Lawrence Weston, Bristol

65

I can remember thinking I'm going to have to try really hard to get a job, but I never thought I wouldn't find one, even though there weren't many around. I had everyone's dream of going into the army, but after thinking about it I realised that if I couldn't bear the regime in school, I certainly shouldn't join the army!

Geoff Clark, aged 18, Bodmin, Cornwall

The careers wife came to school and told us about how to sign on the dole, and what to do if you got a job. As soon as I left, I had a card to take to the careers centre, but there were no jobs so I had to sign on the dole. There was nowt else to do.

Keith Shoulder, aged 17, Elswick, Newcastle-upon-Tyne

I wanted to do a nursery nurse's course, but I didn't have the qualifications, so I decided to try for a hotel receptionist's course. Before I finished the course I'd started writing off to hotels for jobs. I've written 200 letters all over the country. I've been to London a couple of times for interviews, to Oxford, Birmingham and Lichfield, but so far, no luck. I've felt like giving up, but if you do give up you don't stand a chance.

Helen Ashworth, aged 18, Sutton Coldfield, West Midlands

'I didn't even know how to fill in a claimant's form'

When I left school I didn't even know how to fill in a claimant's form. I think they should teach you how to do that while you're still at school, because that's what you've got to do when you leave. It's part of being grown-up. Some people leave school, go straight on the dole and think, 'I'm getting money for nothing,' which is wrong, because it ain't the reason: it's because they don't know enough, because they haven't been educated enough. For them, the world outside the classroom has been non-existent.

John Masefield, aged 19, Kingstanding, Birmingham

The school helped a bit. I knew I wanted to get into the car trade and they gave me phone numbers to ring up, but my Dad found me the job in the end. I'd always been interested in watching him tinker with his car. I'd have liked to do that in school, but they never did car mechanics.

Martin Yates, aged 18, Kingstanding, Birmingham

I didn't have a clue what I wanted to do. I knew I'd go straight on the dole. Careers teachers weren't much good, and all the Headmaster believed in was that you'd be punished in hell — but you can have a detention for now!

Lise Palme, aged 17, Bodmin, Cornwall

Schools could help more with application forms. When I left and forms were put in front of me, I used to think, 'Durr!' — not 'cos I'm simple, but because I didn't know where to start. I can fill in the bit that says, Name, Date of Birth, and Address, but after that I'm lost. A lot of teachers think that the sooner they can get rid of this lot of kids the better. But that just makes us more thick when it comes to going into the world.

Carole Conway, aged 17, St Austell, Cornwall

A lot of kids leave school with plenty of education, but their minds are all mixed up; they don't know what they want. When I was in school I used to see all the stuff about different jobs, but I never knew what I wanted to be. I think I wanted to be a doctor, a magician. . . ! In Guyana though they don't give you much help to find a job; they don't teach you as much as schools over here.

Carl Benjamin, aged 20, Easton, Bristol

Part 2 — Leaving school

'I went all over the place on my pushbike looking for jobs'

The day I left school me and my mates scratched our names on the wall, turned desks around, took numbers off doors and put them on other doors — that sort of thing. It was fun and when we got outside the gates the first thing we did was have a fag. But it was such an anti-climax leaving school. Through the fifth year we'd been counting away the months and days; we'd been thinking, 'In a couple of hours we'll be left, we won't have to come back to this dump again.' But after three or four weeks you wish you were back, because there's nothing to do.

When you're in school you're actually quite secure. I used to get £2 a week pocket money and it used to last me through the week, but when I left I was getting £11 dole money and it never used to last me. It was a wide-awakening sort of thing. You were on your own and had to find things out for yourself. In school you can pick and choose who you work with and who you sit by. When you go out to work you could be working with the biggest creep, and you have no choice at all. I don't think school prepared you for that!

After five weeks I found a job with the Council — a government

67

training scheme. From the Council I went to STD Joineries and was there for six months doing a *real* job — stacking wood. The cut wood came off a conveyor belt and I'd pick it up and put it into a pallet. That's all I was doing every day. Very exciting I got a lot of job satisfaction, but it was either that or the dole and I was earning £29. Then a stack of wood fell on my feet and I was on crutches for a month. I had physiotherapy and all that sort of stuff. When I went back I worked for just one week and detested every minute of it, so I thought, 'I ain't working here any more.' I gave in me notice and left.

I felt great walking out of there. It was even better than leaving school because I *really* hated the job. It was worse than school. The blokes down there would sit in the same place in the crib room each day; they used to take the same sandwiches to work and take the same paper. It was like bloody clockwork. I suppose that's what factories do for you, and I don't want to end up like that.

Marcel Rosari, aged 18, St Austell, Cornwall

All the careers had to offer were shop jobs or in the mill. I would have gone on a YOP scheme doing building, but it meant I had to go to technical college and I thought that would be just like school. Teachers did nowt about jobs for us lot from Bonsall. On our last day at school I sat in the library and read a book and then they called us into the hall for a meeting and said they hoped we'd get on all right. My form teacher said he'd help us, but he never did. I felt a bit let down.

That was three years ago.

I went all over the place on my pushbike looking for jobs. One place said, 'We ain't got nowt yet but we'll let you know,' and they never let me know. I went for one down in Cromford where they fit exhausts, but four others had been there first. Eventually the careers office told me about a YOP scheme at Matlock Bath for six months. Six or seven weeks after I finished that I went to a garage in Cromford and did another YOP job until this bloke with a small garage asked me to come and work for him. It's one of them jobs I like doing — same as metalwork in school. I'm lucky really. If I got the sack I reckon I wouldn't find another job round here. I'd have to go to Matlock again, and that's a problem if you ain't got transport.

Colin Ryder, aged 19, Bonsall, Derbyshire

When I left I spent the time going round Chelmsford, Maldon, Colchester and Burnham, looking for work. I'd thumb to Chelmsford, for instance, and go straight to the unemployment office. They've got an office next door to where you sign on and they put all the jobs up on the walls, so you go in and say, 'Can you give me some idea of job 179 on the board?' They tell you all about it, where it is, what

qualifications you need, and they ring straight through if you say
you're interested. I've been to a lot of interviews, but three-quarters of
them say,'Don't call us, we'll call you.' The others have said, 'Give us a
ring in a week; we'll keep your name in the book.'

I've gone for a whole range of jobs: as a warehouseman packing
paper, with heating companies, as a landscape gardener, in factories,
as a coalman or dustman — nearly every sort of thing going except
office work because I know I haven't got any qualifications for that.
The important thing is your attitude. You have to keep cool in the back
of your mind when you see interviewers and just look as if you're meeting a new friend. I buggered up a lot of interviews because I was so
edgy that all I said was, 'Yeah, yeah.' I don't try to impress them by
going over the top ar d overdoing it. If they say tidy, clean person in
the advert, I jump into me suit, brush me hair and away I go.

I've been going round for seven months now and the nearest I've
got to a job is, 'Well we've got a few more interviews. I *think* we'll
give you a ring; I *think* there could be a possibility; I *think* there might
be a chance.' I think, I think, I think. They never cheer you up and
say you *have* got a good chance.

                                    Matthew Brown, aged 17, Chelmsford, Essex

At first I was going to go to college. I took me exams and took the test
you need for college before you go in. I passed that and went down to
meet the teachers, which put me right off, because they seemed so
bossy. Then I was out of a job for five months.

I used to babysit on odd days for a little boy down the road, but
most of the time I'd just tidy up for my Mum and go into town to see
if I could see anyone else who was on the dole. I think I went to eleven
interviews without any luck until one day, before I went for an interview at Storeys, the careers bloke said, 'What do you think you're doing
wrong? You don't mind if I say, but I think you might talk a bit too
fast and they may not be able to understand you. Try to talk a bit
slower. You're dressed OK for an interview, just go in smiling, give
them a good impression of what you are, be friendly, and if they say,
"Any questions?" make sure you have something to ask — show them
you're interested.' So when I went to the interview I talked a lot
slower, and that was how I got the government scheme with Storeys. It
was a clerical job, which I really enjoyed.

I was there for five months with four weeks left to go on the
scheme when the careers office phoned me about a full-time job with a
firm of solicitors. I went for an interview and they offered me the job.
I'm an office junior doing typing, deliveries, answering the phone —
everything really. It's a lot different from school. The only time you're
told to do anything is, 'Will you do photocopying?' or, 'Will you take

69

this round?' It's never 'Do it!', it's 'Will you?'

You have to be more independent than when you're at school. You have to learn to do everything yourself and do things at home which your Mum would have done beforehand. I have to pay me board, but after that I can make me own decisions about what I buy. At first I found it hard handling money. I get £32.90 after deductions and I used to spend it all at once. I'd be paid on Friday and be spent up by Tuesday.

Trish Doherty, aged 17, Lancaster

'I've tried getting jobs, but it's the same story every time'

When I left you couldnae sign on until September. That was the hardest bit 'cos you never had any money and my Dad and Mum were both unemployed. Everybody used tae get on each others' nerves because we were seeing too much of each other sitting in the house all the time. I've read much more than I've ever done through the whole of my schooling I think. It's better than sitting watching the telly.

I put applications in for a care assistant in homes working for Lothian Regional Council. I had three offers of interviews, but within the week, all the application forms came back saying 'due to the economic situation they were unable to take on more posts'. All my interviews were cancelled which was really depressing.

Maureen McLaughlin, aged 18, Edinburgh

When I left I found a job in a garage as an apprentice motor mechanic. Then I had an argument with my Mother, so I left home and went to live with my sister, Sheila; but it was too far away to come to work so I packed the job in. I'd worked Saturdays and Sundays when I was at school, in a café in Newcastle, so the boss gave me a full-time job there, but that didn't last long either, because somebody did a burglary and they thought it was me. The person who'd been seen had had a skinhead cut and, since I had a skinhead then, I fitted the description. I had to go to court, but the court case went on for 5½ months before they found out it wasn't me. The police remanded me in custody during that time. It turned out the burglary had been done by Sheila's boyfriend and some other girl with a skinhead cut.

After that my father wouldn't have me back and, since I didn't have anywhere else to stay, they sent me to this children's home. I've tried getting jobs, but it's the same story every time − forty people go for one interview and somebody else gets it. It's usually shop work. I go down every Thursday to the careers office, but with that burglary the police have my name down on record because I was in custody for

5½ months. Employers don't take much to that when I tell them. I don't build my hopes now.

I've thought of going back to school to do A levels, 'cos I passed seven O levels, but I left school so long ago now, that I'm not sure I could.

Beverley Fenwick, aged 17, Whitley Bay, Northumberland

'When you're paid you can put up with it'

I've had several real jobs: working for the Gas Board, digging roads up to lay pipes, and working for a glass fibre firm on the quay. They paid me £60 a week, but it was a lousy job. Now I understand what boredom is: it's doing repetitive work. All we was doing was taking long strands of glass fibre, spreading them out, pulling 'em out, pulling 'em back, folding 'em up, cutting 'em in the middle, rolling 'em up in plastic sheets and throwing them in a pile – doing that all day. After six months I was made redundant. They said they'd give us a word if business started bucking up again, but I haven't heard owt yet. So I'm back on a government scheme earning £23.50 again.

Alan Myerscough, aged 20, Lancaster

My first job was in an import and export factory. It was really boring. I'd be standing there from 9.00 'till 4.00 unwrapping towels from big boxes, and putting them in piles of twos and threes. It was a £1 an hour though, which wasn't so bad. When you're getting paid you can put up with it being boring. If I'd been paid to go to school I'd have gone.

The other difference apart from money, is that they're not so bony at work. They look at you as the same as they are – same age and class, whereas in school teachers would think, 'Oh, kids, boss 'em about.' If you want to go to the toilet in school you have to stick up your hand. At work you go whenever you want to.

Joanne Clark, aged 17, Chelmsford, Essex

After six months on the dole I saw a job in the paper at Fitzgeralds making fluorescent lights and I went along for the interview. He asked me what I'd done before and whether I thought I'd find it interesting, so I said, 'Yeah!' He showed me round the factory and asked me to start on Monday. It was easy. They didn't care who they took on. I was earning £40 a week, but it was like being back at school. I thought, 'I'll stick it out for another six months,' but I couldn't stand the place. I left in January, and didn't get any dole money for six weeks. All I had was a fiver a week that my parents gave me. I couldn't get another job – partly 'cos I've got spiky hair. I could be the most intelligent

71

person in the bleedin' world and still have a grotty appearance. Some
guys in suits are really thick.

Lise Palme, aged 17, Bodmin, Cornwall

I left after my exams and worked with my Mum on an egg farm picking
up eggs. There's other people on the farm, but it's only the two of us
who collect eggs. I can have a day off any time I like to look after my
baby — except when they're really busy. It's boring work, but it's
better than sitting at home. I don't want to look for a full-time job or
think about a government scheme, because I want time to be with my
baby.

I'll look for a different job when she's five and starts school. I don't
particularly want to stay around picking up eggs for years on end. I'd
really like to work with kids. When I was at school I did work experience in a play group. I love children and animals. I'd have liked to be
a teacher, but I'm not brainy enough.

Ronny Moore, aged 17, Southminster, Essex

The first job I took was as a dental nurse, but I didnae like the man I
was working for. I didnae have any respect for him. I didnae like the
way he treated his patients or the way he treated me in front of his
patients. He had no integrity.

He owned a hotel in Edinburgh and I had tae wait until the first
patient was in, then phone him at his hotel tae tell him. Because it
took him 45 minutes to come up from Edinburgh we were three-
quarters of an hour behind schedule right at the start. Then he'd be
harassed because he had a long line of patients that had been waiting
for ages. People would come in for a check-up and he always gave a
filling. By four o'clock in the afternoon you had about ten people
in the waiting room. He'd be really agitated then and because he
couldnae cope with it he'd start shouting at me in front of patients.
So I gave it up after two months.

Jacquie Irving, aged 17, Edinburgh

'In school you can mess about, but you can't at work'

The difference between school and a job is that at work you accept the
fact that you've got to do something you're told to do, because you're
getting paid for it.

David Purves, aged 16, Edinburgh

In school you can mess about, but you can't at work. At school you're
all the same age, but at work they're in their thirties and forties and

they treat me as a kid. I have to take a lot of stick like looking for left handed screw-drivers.

Robert Morris, aged 17, Sutton Coldfield, West Midlands

I felt that I'd grown up and was self-supporting. I'd meet friends and they'd say, 'Coming out tonight?' and I could turn round and say, 'Yeah, smashing,' without having to worry about cash. If someone had said that to me at school I'd think they were having me on. At work you're closer to people – even the ones telling you what to do. If I didn't know how to operate a machine, I'd go up and ask the manager, or if I'd done a job wrong, I could go up and say, 'Look, I've done this wrong, can you correct it?' In school if you get something wrong and you go up to the teacher and say, 'Can you correct this?' he'd say, 'I haven't the time just now.' It's a different atmosphere altogether.

John Masefield, aged 19, Kingstanding, Birmingham

'As long as I enjoy it, the money doesn't matter'

I expect to be treated like a human being. I'd like the boss to treat me more as a friend than an employee. I don't mind working long hours and I'm not all that interested in a lot of money. As long as I enjoy it, the money doesn't matter. As a forklift truck driver I quite enjoy it, but I'm not really that conscientious about it.

I think it's good if the job means more than just the money, but the way management treat people has a great deal to do with it. When they treat you like dirt and don't give a damn whether you're there or not, then it snowballs onto you. You treat the factory like dirt, or you don't give a damn what you're doing, as long as you're getting the money at the end of the week.

I just do as I'm told and think nothing of it, or I think about other things, like going off for the day somewhere. I'll be driving along thinking what it'd be like if I owned the company. Perhaps I'd sell the place and keep the money.

Gordon MacMillan, aged 23, Baptist Mills, Bristol

The most important thing for me is friendship. An office full of women is so bitchy, it's really nasty. You have to fight to break down those barriers.

Catherine Crowe, aged 17, Wardley, West Midlands

Young people's comments

'I'd rather be on the dole than be miserable'

Being with people I genuinely like, without having to pretend that I get on with them, is the most important thing; not just doing a job for the sake of the money, but actually enjoying it and feeling satisfied when I've done something. Some people don't mind working in a factory, but it would drive me barmy after one day. If I worked in a factory and was really miserable, I think I'd much rather be on the dole.

Jo Chadwick, aged 17, Trowbridge, Wilts

People do jobs just for the money, but I need to be really satisfied with what I'm doing for me to think it's a good job. The lucky people are those who have a job that they're satisfied with *and* enjoy doing. They work quicker and achieve more. Money's not important to me now, although it was when I first left school.

I wouldn't like to work in a factory just to earn £70 a week. I don't think I'd ever go for that sort of job. If I had the chance of a job for £30 a week outside and a £70 a week factory job, I'd probably go for the job outside.

Geoff Clark, aged 18, Bodmin, Cornwall

The trouble is these days that if you don't like any of the choices for jobs, there's nothing else you can do.

You want *something*, but you don't know what the heck it is, because you ain't found it so far. If you're handed a list of all the jobs that are going and you don't like any of them, what do you do? Christ knows; I don't.

Caroline Asquith, aged 16, Easton, Bristol

See pp. 134-8 for the response by Andrew Bird.

Chapter 6

The search for work

Part 1 – Some personal experiences

'You were covered in blood from head to foot'

I really wanted to work at the Zoo, but our Ma fixed up my first job
where two of me brothers were working down Avonmouth, sorting
hides. All you had was the skin with the hairs and the tail left on and it
was our job to trim them, weigh them, sort them and stack them.

It was a vile job. You were covered in blood from head to foot, and
I cut myself with the knives a couple of times 'cos they was razor sharp.
There were little worms in the hides and, if they got into your cuts,
they made your cuts swell. The worst part was having to keep handling
salt because with these cuts all over me hands, they was stinging all day
long. You had to salt the hides so they wouldn't go off.

I was there five months. They took me on 'cos my two brothers
were working there really well, so they thought I would too. Unfortunately I was the one who didn't give a damn. A friend of mine told me
about another job in UKAY so I went to see about that and the boss
there said I could start anytime. So I handed me notice in down the
hide market, went to UKAY but he'd already filled the job. So I had
nowhere to go except on the dole. They wouldn't have taken me back
and I wouldn't have gone back anyway since I hated the job so much.

By then the Zoo had written to say there was no vacancies, and
wouldn't be in the near future. Then I really didn't know where to
turn. You just had to go around and hope that, if you saw a job you
might be interested in, you might get it to see what it's like. Not long
after that I became keen on being a postman. But I kept failing the
maths test. You have a test – initiative, a bit of English and a bit of
maths – and maths I failed on.

I've never really bothered about money. Since I left school all I wanted to do was get a job I was really interested in. That's why when I left school I was trying for almost a year to get in the Zoo. There *was* a job going in the Zoo but I was eighteen when it came up and they only wanted someone as young as seventeen; so it did come up, but it came up a year too late.

Andy James, aged 20, Lawrence Weston, Bristol

'I'd like to have my own boutique now'

I worked in an office for a year after I left. When I went for the interview I'd thought what a beautiful place to work, but the supervisor never showed me around, and when I started on the Monday she took me downstairs to this dull, dim office with no windows. It was a microfilm company and they taught us how to use the cameras, and how to file invoices and documents on microfilm. It wasn't what I'd expected. I'd expected to be sitting at a desk, typing away, because they'd asked for a filing clerk.

I felt treated the same as at school. You had your tea break at 3.00 and if you weren't back by ten minutes past you were in trouble. The supervisor worked upstairs and if you heard her footsteps, you ran back to your desk. I enjoyed it at first 'cos I was away from school, but after a while I used to wake up in the morning and think 'Oh no! Another day at work. Yuck!'

After a year I decided I must leave.

Before I'd left school I'd had a Saturday job in a boutique for extra money. I went down there one night feeling really miserable and Mrs Monroe who owned it was feeling miserable too, because her assistant had just left and she asked me if I would like to work full-time for her. I said, 'Great, this has given me the answer I need.' I gave up my office job straight away and I've been with her ever since. I love it. I've always had an interest in fashion, but I never ever thought I'd work in a boutique. I thought I'd always be in an office.

Sometimes even in the shop I feel like screaming. If you get a lady in and you drag everything out and she starts complaining and moaning it does get you down a bit, but if you enjoy it as much as I do you don't really think about it. When I see all the different fashions going in and out over the years, I realise how much things have changed. Mrs Monroe gives me a certain amount of responsibility, because she often asks me to tell Sylvia, the other assistant who works part-time, to do this and do that. I actually have to tell somebody under me what to do. I don't really mind, but I always think Sylvia's going to take offence if I tell her to do something — because I've never had to do that before.

Over the years I've seen how Mrs Monroe runs the shop. She always introduces me to the salesmen and I answer a lot of the telephone calls. She's taught me the ropes. I'd like to have my own boutique now.

Audrey Nelson, aged 18, Edinburgh

'All I could hear was the cracking of bones'

I left at Easter and found a job almost straight away. It was in Avonmouth, dealing with protective clothing – warehouse work. I was there for two months, doing really well, except for a knock with the boss's Princess. He went scatty; it was about £90 worth of damage. I didn't get the sack but I had to pay so much for it out of my wages. Then I heard about another warehouse job in Avonmouth. I rang 'em up and they asked me to come down and offered me the job straight away. I told my boss I was leaving – and said, 'The money I owe you for the car, could you take it from my holiday money?' He was all for that.

I started on the following Monday. It was the same work as I'd been doing before but this time I was dealing with food. In the second week I was due my first week's pay of £40, which wasn't bad for a sixteen-year-old, but on the Thursday I had an accident on the fork-lift truck that I drove sometimes. I was painting a refrigerator trailer using the fork of the truck like a ladder, and as I finished each panel I had to climb down to release the lever to lower the forks. I was painting way until it was time for dinner. Then I started climbing down by holding onto the forks. I put my left leg down and caught it on the lever which releases the hydraulics. The next thing I knew was the machinery coming down on top of my hand. I shouted out for help and was beeping the horn. There was nothing else I could do. I could hear a crackling from my wrist. It seemed like ages before somebody came. I'd begun to give up hope and was wondering where they all were.

The first guy who came out thought I was joking but when he came up to me he said 'Jesus Christ' and ran off. It was bedlam; everyone was running, wondering what to do. They had to call the fire brigade to cut me out because my hand was stuck in a certain position. I was rushed to hospital. It was only afterwards that I had the pain. I didn't feel a thing when the chains came down on me hand. All I could hear was the cracking of bones – sometimes I still hear it now. The ambulance men gave me gas to kill the pain.

I can use my hand again now. It's not too bad, although it's deformed and I haven't got the grip I used to have. Now and again it becomes really weak when I'm writing or playing badminton. I can be playing for ten minutes, then, without warning, it loses grip.

Chris Rich, aged 18, Easton, Bristol

'I was selling semi-precious stones'

I left school on Friday and started work on the following Monday as
an assistant selling semi-precious stones. My Mother had seen the advert
and suggested I tried for it. Six others had applied, but they chose me,
probably because I was a school leaver and they wanted someone young
around the office to learn the trade.

When I started I didn't know anything about stones, but as the
months went by I loved working there. I was meeting people over the
counter, writing letters and invoices and answering the phone. It was a
good atmosphere. People there were so friendly. I felt a bit lonely at
first, but I was introduced to everyone, and all the girls started talking
to me — and would ask how I was getting on and help sort out any
problems. Everyone did that — help each other out. That was one thing
very different to school.

Some things were the same as school — like having a boss instead of
a Headmaster. You also had rules and regulations though not so many
as at school. I got on well with the boss. We had motor bikes in
common, you see, and he used to talk to me. I never had anything in
common with the Headmaster. When I started work I was the youngest
in the firm, but I was on the trade counter and people would come in
and talk to me like to anyone else. It made me feel great, because at
school I'd just been regarded as one of the kids. The other difference
is that you get money for a job. Though it's like school in the sense
that you have to do it, you do actually get paid at the end of the week.

After nine months I was made redundant, because of the recession.
No one would buy big stones any more. I was out of work for months
before I found a job in a photo-developing laboratory on a two-week
trial basis. You had to do something like five hundred prints in a day,
all one at a time with the right colouring. Each print took a minute
each. I managed to get up to four hundred by the end of the fortnight,
which was near enough the mark, but they said, 'Sorry you're not quick
enough.' I said I'd pick up speed if I was there a while longer. It's like
typing; you can't learn to type in two weeks. But it was no use. I don't
know what they expected from me — to be superwoman I think.

I was back on the dole.

I'm still going for interviews, though I feel like giving up sometimes.
My Mum buys the paper. We go down the job pages.

'Oh that looks good — ring up.'

'Well, the job's been taken.'

'How can it be taken when it was only put in this afternoon?'

'They probably had a relation who was unemployed, so put them
in the job rather than interview anybody else.'

And then you see jobs that say Male/Female, but when you go along

they say, 'Well, we really want a male — we just had to put male or female in the paper 'cos it's the law.' Or it says, 'Experience not essential,'
but when you go there they're looking for someone with experience.
And a hell of a lot of jobs say twenty-one or over. It's no wonder
people give up trying.

Ley Alberici, aged 17, Great Barr, Birmingham

'It'll go up at eighteen if I become a frier'

My Dad said to me, 'No one in this house has ever been on the dole so
if you can't find a job in the summer holidays you're going back to
school!'

I tried pretty hard to find a job. I had a little book in which I used
to write all the dates, the name of the personnel manager wherever I'd
been and what the reply was — whether it was 'to come back', or 'no
thank you', or 'we'll phone you, don't phone us'. I used to cycle round
all the shops and factories, and I'd look in the *Evening Telegraph* in
the evenings or go down to the Job Centre. I was into dogs at the time
and wanted to work in kennels, so I bought a kennel magazine. In the
back they list places that offered jobs, so I went through that. It cost
me about three new tyres, but I couldn't find a job! That took up most
of the summer.

I was too young to be left at home as far as me Mum and Dad were
concerned so I had to stop to go on holiday. But I kept on looking even
when I was on holiday in Cornwall. The way I was feeling by then, if
I'd seen anything there I would have done it. Everything's on top of
you. Your Mum and Dad are nagging and saying, 'I don't think you can
be trying or you'd have one by now.' You begin to think they're not
seeing the world as it is and it makes you angry. I was feeling a bit un-
steady by then — and there were quite a few times when I tried killing
my little brother. I actually began to think I was going barmy.

I was hoping like crazy that I wouldn't have to go back to school,
because all my friends had left. But I had to in the end, and when I
did, I'd avoid using the word 'school' if I was talking with my mates
because they'd be embarrassed to be with someone who was still at
school. I tried to keep it a secret and say things like, 'I've got to be in
by 9.00 a.m.' when they asked me what time I started!

I took more exams at the end of the year, but I didn't do any better.
It wasn't a waste of a year though, because I changed a lot in myself.
It gave me a chance to grow up more.

The end of the year came and I was in a panic because me Dad
would have tanned my hide for being the first one in the family on
the dole. But just before schools went back I had a phone call from

the chip shop and they said I'd got the job. I put the phone down and screamed me head off. Me Mum gave me a quid because she'd had a bet that I couldn't get a job by the end of the week. It was terrific. It wasn't a fantastic job, but at least I'd got a job and I was something.

Now I'm working in there, people come in and say, 'Hello Cheryl.' They all know my name. It's like working in a pub; you get your regulars. There's tons of people I know by face who'll talk to me and who I'd have thought of before as being grown-up. When I was at school, if you were seen talking to a policeman that was something really bad, and if you were told off by one you were great for a week. But after you've been working in a chip shop and you hear someone talking about 'The Fuzz' or 'The Pigs' you think they're really stupid. The police come round at night if we think there's someone standing outside the front door, and they'll wait around in the back. Now I wave to policemen; it's great to see one.

I've learnt *some* skills in these five months. Before I worked there I wouldn't have known how the heck to do batter – 'cos it's not like you do it at home. And there's the fish – you have to stack them in a certain way. There's the frying, like how long you can leave the chips in; there's beef burgers and the onions. It's not just boiling the onions – you have to put in something special to give them a nice taste. Or there's the pickled eggs, you have to learn how long to leave them in the drawer before you can bring them out and put them on sale. I'm earning about £45 a week. It'll go up at eighteen depending on whether I become a frier or not.

Cheryl Davidson, aged 17, Bretton, Peterborough

'I went digging for gold and diamonds'

When I left, I worked with my Father in Guyana before starting something rather like a TOPS course. After two years though I'd had enough of training in different trades and I wanted a real job. I did garage work, dock work and panel beating, but I wasn't learning much and the pay wasn't very good. So then I went digging for gold and diamonds and that wasn't any better because you only had enough money to last until you were ready to go back in and dig for more gold and diamonds.

You don't find them just like that; you can't just pick them up like rocks or eggs. They're deep underneath the sand. At the bottom of the sand is a black substance like dirt, and mixed with that is the gold and diamonds. It's very, very thin like sand grains, so when you take it up it's of no immediate value. You need a kit to extract it by different processes of straining. After that it's still no good, so you have to melt it together and after that you can bring it to town and sell it, and you have to give the government some of the profit. But however much money you made it wasn't really enough because the cost of living is so high. Things like clothes are really dear.

It's harder in Guyana. It's more difficult to find jobs and when you do find them you have to work harder. From twelve to four the sun is at its highest, and it's really burning if you have to work outside all day. It drains all your energy but you still have to work. The foreman doesn't say, 'Take a rest every fifteen minutes.'

If black guys leaving school in England said they wanted to go back to Jamaica I'd say, 'Go ahead.' They have to see for themselves that it's harder. Maybe they'll be lucky and want to stay. So they need to experience it for themselves.

My parents thought Guyana would be better than England and they left their house and jobs here because they reckoned they'd do better in Guyana. They lost all their money and now it's too late for them to come back to England, even if they could afford it. They can't say, 'I'm gonna start a TOPS course' because by the time they're ready for employment people would say, 'No over-nineties!'

Over there, when people listen and hear you speak a bit foreign, they ask why you don't go back to England, why you're so stupid to have come to Guyana! Black people over here don't realise that the enemy isn't just white people. They've got enemies within their race, within their family. Black people over here just think the whites alone are their enemy. It's different in Guyana. Black people own the firms and most of them are controlled by the Prime Minister. You can only get a job by going to certain black people and they're bound to give them to their friends first. You have to join the government party protecting the Prime Minister and give him half of your salary if you want a job — and he will tell you how much you can take home to your family and what your work conditions are like.

If a white person goes to Guyana he gets treated all right, but a black person will have to fend for himself. When my Father went back he was just ordinary, so he had to go and suffer and lose all his money without help from his family. If he'd been a white person they'd have treated him nice because they think they might get treated nice when they go to England. It's funny, but if a black person in Guyana or Jamaica gets treated bad by a black person he feels like killing him but if he gets treated bad by a white person in England he accepts it up to a point because he can see his skin is a different colour, so he expects it. There's much more violence in Guyana and more rioting than in England.

Carl Benjamin, aged 20, Easton, Bristol

Young people's comments

Part 2 – On the dole

'I thought it would be great to be paid to do nothing but . . .'

I went up to London to work in a book shop. I took my exams and left about three days after. I was working as a secretary but I didn't like London because I didn't know anybody so I came back at Christmas. Then I went on the dole for nearly eight months. I had a job in a kitchen for a week until they laid us all off. They hadn't told us they were going to do that.

It was good fun for the first couple of months 'cos I had a friend who was on the dole as well but she went away to Kent and I was on my own. On the dole on your own definitely isn't any fun. After a while you get fed up having no money, and being pestered by the DHSS. I did look for jobs. I went to the Job Centre but there was nothing, except factory work or something where you had to have transport, which is a major problem round here. In summer there's hotel work going but nothing in winter. Sometimes we'd go down the pub in the evenings, buy half a lager and make it last all night. At the end of the evening we'd still have half of a half a lager left! We were that bored, we'd much rather sit in the pub and watch people than watch TV.

Maxine Irving, aged 17, Camelford, Cornwall

I thought it would be really great being paid to do nothing. I was lucky, because I had a girl friend, so I didn't really need to go out that much. But I feel sorry for the people who don't, especially if they've got their Gran at home as well as their parents. I worked for my Dad for a bit. He's a painter and decorator, but then my Mum and Dad split up and he moved to Bristol. Then I took a summer job in Woolies, but they sacked me. I found something and thought no one had seen me, but I was being watched.

I had to go on the dole. I really regretted it. They don't offer you jobs; you just go to collect your money and everyone at the dole office treats you like a criminal. When I went down there and said I'd like to claim supplementary benefit, he asked why I left my job. When I said I'd been in trouble and been sacked, he said, 'Well that's your fault isn't it? You won't be able to claim here for six weeks.' I said I'd apply anyway 'cos you can get a form to fight against it. He said it was a waste of time and not to bother. I said, 'What am I supposed to do for six weeks if I don't have any money?'

Dylan Williams, aged 17, Newquay, Cornwall

When I stopped work I used to have nightmares about unwrapping towels. For the first week it was just lovely to be away from the place. Then it got boring, because there wasn't anything to get up for. I'd lie in bed till two o'clock or so, really bored. I couldn't sign on straight away and, since I hate asking my Mum for money, I didn't have any cash to spend. Now they send me £30.50 every two weeks and I give me Mum £20.00 which leaves me £5 a week.

I've given up looking for jobs. I used to get up early quite a few mornings and look in the paper to see if I could find anything before anyone else. But for jobs in the paper you need to be qualified and 18 or 21. It's the same down the Job Centre.

I worked in the Wimpy for a little while. It was part-time night work at £1.18 an hour, but God, the boss didn't half make you work for it. I worked from 5.00 to 10.45 p.m. and he'd let you sit down once in that time for ten minutes, so your legs nearly fell off by the end of the night. Then we used to have to bleach the whole shop down and fill all the sauce bottles. I didn't mind the hard work. I just didn't like the boss. I've been on the dole for a couple of months now. Me Mum goes away at weekends from Friday night to Sunday mornings, so I clean up and cook me brother's dinner and me boy friend's, cos he stays round at the weekend. I do the Hoovering up, cleaning the windows and ironing. She leaves it tidy when she goes, but me brothers are like little kids even though one of them is fifteen and the other's thirteen.

I've thought of doing CSV. I know the money's low, but I'd like to do something with kids. It's all right if they're not your own 'cos if they get on your nerves you can send them back to where they come from. I'm getting £15 at the moment for doing nothing, but I'd rather have £10 for doing something on CSV. Doing nothing just drives you up the wall.

Joanne Clark, aged 17, Chelmsford, Essex

I hope I'm never unemployed again because I don't like being out of a job. The first few days are great: you can get on and do the things you always wanted to do. But after a week or two you're bored, you're depressed and you feel guilty. I don't know why, but I feel I should be working. When you go down the Social Security places you're sitting there with people who don't really want to be working, people who drink, people who are not interested in getting a job as long as they can get their money, and I think why bother if they're not going to bother.

Gordon MacMillan, aged 23, Baptist Mills, Bristol

Young people's comments

'I felt sympathy for the kids rioting'

I felt a bit of sympathy for the kids rioting, because I know what it's like myself. They're bored up to the eyeballs. With the money off the labour they can buy clothes and pay for their keep but that's all. I pay £20 out of £38 a fortnight. That leaves me £18. If I have to buy a pair of shoes that's the rest gone. I don't think I'd smash windows myself, but you don't really know till the time comes. If I was walking up a street with shop windows smashed in, people would say, 'You're an idiot walking past.'

I've been for thirty or forty jobs that I've seen in the paper, or at the Job Centre. Each one I've been to they say they'll let you know through the post, and you don't hear a thing. Some times the job had gone already when I got there, because the Job Centre hadn't checked the files. That makes me angry. Once I walked from Coronation Street, where I sign on, to Bristow's for an interview, which the Job Centre had suggested: eight miles altogether and the job had gone; there wasn't a vacancy at all. The Job Centre had told me they'd phoned up beforehand. It made me mad to think I'd walked all that way and not had anything to eat or drink, and the job had been gone for two or three weeks. I'd walked because I only had enough fare for signing on and getting home again.

It worries me when I think I'm going to be out of work for quite a while yet. I get depressed just walking around the streets, trying to pass the time, until I go home and go to bed. Then I get up and it's another day. I don't stay in bed late, because I sleep with my brother who has to go out to work at 7 a.m. and his alarm wakes me up. Some days I help out at Frenchay Park doing odd jobs, but they can't pay me and, even if they could, I'm not qualified for the job.

John Masefield, aged 19, Kingstanding, Birmingham

If you can't find a job you go on the dole; there's not much choice is there? I've been brought up to expect it. I was on the dole seven months after leaving school. I started off by getting up early, but after two months I used to lie in till about eleven o'clock. Our Mum would wake me when she went off to work 'cos I'd be the only one in the house. I'd have a cup of tea and some breakfast, play records, then I'd go to this café that opened about a year and a half ago, sit there and spend 60p. I worked out that I could spend so much a day on machines and a cup of tea. Mondays, Tuesdays, Thursdays and Fridays I'd go down the Youth Club, but a kid nicked the record player so there was only table tennis and snooker. Everyone stopped going then, so I'd come home and watch telly. If there was a concert in town I'd stay in the house all week and save up. At first I thought it *was* going to end,

then I thought what's going to happen is going to happen, so there ain't
much I can do about it. I sort of gave up, but my record collection
helped in a way: stuff like 'Blank Generation' and 'Pretty Fatal' by The
Pistols – 'You're treated like shit, but you don't have to be shit because
they think you're shit.' I read some books like *The Boy looked at
Johnny* about some punks, which is a really good book.

I read a letter in a magazine last week by a girl who'd written about
the two kids killing themselves (20 September 1981), saying how silly
it was because she'd been like that once. She'd been on the dole for
thirteen months and it had ruined her social life so she ran away to
London and it changed everything; but she said, 'You haven't necessarily got to run away to London, you've got to find your own way out
of your own rut. It's easy to say: "Oh, I'm on the dole, that's the
problem", or "I live in a shit area", but you have to realise that the
problem is how you see yourself. If you realise that it's yourself it'll
change things.' It may sound silly but once you realise *that*, your whole
outlook changes; that's what happend to me; I started thinking that *I*
was the problem and the only way to change it was to change myself. I
started thinking, 'I'm not going to try and fit in just to make my life
easier; I'm going to stick with what I think. If nobody likes it then it's
tough shit, I'll go it on my own.' When I'd first gone down the careers
I had long spiky hair and they said I'd never get a job looking like that,
so I cut it off really short. But after thinking things through and reading
what that girl had said, I thought I ain't going to cut my hair off again.
Then when they said I could have a job at Boots, I said, 'I don't want a
job at Boots, you *know* I want a job with art.' When they sent me on a
course about how to find a job, there were kids doing things like
changing plugs. If that had been before, I'd have fitted in, but instead I
said, 'No, I ain't doing that – that's pathetic.' That was when they
suggested Bush Telegraph – this YOP scheme – and I found that
people here had the same views as me, so I stayed on.

Ray Scanlon, aged 17, Lawrence Weston, Bristol

I wouldn't go to the extent of rioting just because I haven't got a job.
I can see the point of a lot of coloured people rioting, because of preju-
dice when they go for a job and the boss looks at them and thinks,
'We're not going to have his type here in this factory.'

Ley Alberici, aged 17, Great Barr, Birmingham

'Not even Superman could get us out of this mess'

It's most lonely about three to four o'clock, just before people come
home, because you've been on your own all day. If your family's

working it's better because they come home and start talking about what sort of day they've had at work! It must be worse if the whole family is on the dole, sitting there with glum faces.

Andrew Seal, aged 19, Great Barr, Birmingham

I make things out of pegs sometimes. My Father's got a 'Do it yourself' manual and I picked up the idea from that. I buy clothes pegs and make models in the evenings by taking the springs out and joining them together. I've made rocking chairs and now I'm working on a trailer for a shire horse that someone gave me.

Philip Drew, aged 17, St Austell, Cornwall

You see all your mates at school taking their O and A levels, and you begin to wish you'd stayed on. I think they should leave the door open for six to twelve months so that if you find you don't like working life, you can go back and try and get some more qualifications.

My mates without a job are bored and fed up. They try hard, but they think they're never going to find a job. I think that's why there's so much vandalism. People say, 'I wonder why vandals do this and do that?' but it's sheer boredom. With nothing to do all day, they're very frustrated: 'Let's go down the park and smash a few bottles.' Sounds stupid, but it's quite easy to feel like that when you're bored. They think they've a right to work but since the situation isn't going to change at all, there's nothing much they can do about it. They're bright lads you see. They look hard. They go to the Job Centre every day. But we're in a right mess now. Not even Superman could get us out of this situation.

Robert Morris, aged 17, Sutton Coldfield, West Midlands

'You're not really trying'

I think being on the dole still has a social stigma attached to it. I know there are a lot of people on the dole, but a lot of other people still regard you as a failure if you haven't got a job. But there just aren't the jobs. My friend's been on the dole for over a year. She's tried for jobs and been for interviews, and nothing's happened.

Tracy Atkinson, aged 16, Longbenton, Newcastle-upon-Tyne

My friend was out of work for nearly three years and all she wanted to do after that was get married.

Catherine Crowe, aged 17, Wardley, West Midlands

I'm fed up now thinking I might not find a job. The first couple of interviews I'd sit waiting for a letter offering me the job. I just thought it'd be easy. But I'd either receive no letter at all or one saying I hadn't got the job. At first I was upset when a job said 'No', but now I forget about it, so I suppose I've changed a bit since leaving school. I still hope that they'll say, 'Come for an interview,' or that I've been short-listed, but I don't think that's going to happen yet.

It really irritates me when I hear older people say that young people who are unemployed aren't trying to find a job. People ask me if I've found a job yet and then say, 'Well, you're not really trying.' They don't know how many letters I write a week. They're sitting comfortably in their jobs, and they think it's easy — but it's not.

Heather Crompton, aged 18, Great Barr, Birmingham

It was OK for a while. I wasn't bored. I was doing what I wanted to do — reading and playing records. I read a lot of Tolkien. I saw friends from school who were also looking for jobs. I went for interviews, but it would fizzle out because I wasn't interested in what they were offering. I knew what I didn't want to do, which was work in a factory. I think to do that you have to kind of anaesthetise yourself, which I know I can't do.

I tried interviews for about six months and by then I realised that life on the dole wasn't so bad, because I actually enjoyed spending days reading and listening to music. I play a bit on the guitar but mostly on my own since I'm not confident enough to play with other people I know.

I must have spent about two years on the dole, until the people who were dishing out money became very heavy every time I went to sign on. Then I started to feel a bit guilty and knew it was time to do something else, so I came on a YOP Scheme.

A lot of people were saying that I ought to work, that I owed society something, but I don't understand the value placed on work. People make it the be-all and end-all of life: the thing you've got to do from sixteen to sixty-five, or whenever you retire.

I know you need to give something but I was doing some writing when I was on the dole — poetry and stuff. That was my contribution. Maybe I could scrape by on it; it would be work, but work that I'd chosen to do. Usually when I write something, I'm indifferent to it, but occasionally I do something that I'm really pleased with. I can show it to people, but I can't read it out myself.

Barrie McGovern, aged 21, Bodmin, Cornwall

Young people's comments

'Guys who don't work slip into shady deals'

Guys who don't work slip into shady deals — like car mechanics un-registered, or acting as middle men for stolen stuff. I think girls get married and become housewives, and then don't have to worry about work 'cos they've got kids round their necks. It's a way out if you can't find a job.

Kerry Parkes, aged 21, Great Barr, Birmingham

When I stopped the first job, I thought I'd have a couple of days' rest — maybe a week — before getting another job, but it's not as easy as that. After the first week when you can't find a job you get a bit worried, and wonder how long it's going to be before you do find one. During the day you are sleeping until two o'clock, watching telly in the afternoon, going out at night and coming in at all hours. Your whole life system's changed. After a month maybe you turn to crime — screwing parking meters or mucking about. I think the government *could* do something, like getting school leavers to make things for countries abroad, where there's a lot of poverty and illness. It'd be useful at least.

David Purves, aged 16, Edinburgh

It's a'right at first, but if your mates are working and you see them getting more money, you realise that if you had a proper job you'd be getting more money too. But there's no permanent jobs at all round here, except for people with A levels.

The thing that really gets you down is having the police on your back everywhere you gang. If someone's broken in a house they'll pick you up because they have to nail somebody. The police have got a grudge on people around here — because there's been a lot of violence.

I've done *some* things I've been caught for, and I've done *some* things I haven't been caught for, but now I'm being pulled in for things I haven't done. In court they'll always take the policeman's word. Sometimes they get rough when you won't tell them what they want to know; they put you in the cell and give you a hiding. If you say you've done it, they won't hit you, but you regret it after-wards, because you're gonna get charged for it and you don't want to be called a grass.

Nobody likes the 'Bizzies' round here.

Keith Shoulder, aged 17, Elswick, Newcastle-upon-Tyne

I've lots of friends who are still unemployed. One of them doesn't think anything about it; he doesn't try. He was on a job training course, but he kept pinching stuff. Now he doesn't bother; he sleeps and watches telly. Some of the others have given up, because they've gone down the Job Centre and found nothing there.

Martin Yates, aged 18, Kingstanding, Birmingham

'Even if another year passes, I'll still keep trying'

I was on the dole for seven weeks. I ain't got a Dad 'cos he went away, so I helped me Mum by decorating the house. She works at Westfarmer Rubber – putting the rubber pieces inside syringes. When I'd finished the decorating I'd wander into town or go and see friends, but I didn't have much money because I gave most of it to my Mum. I helped her with the cooking and cleaning as well, and realised for the first time how hard housework is.

Andrew Pearce, aged 16, St Austell, Cornwall

I was always doing something, but I was fed up about not having a job or some money in my pocket to do more things. I was helping people here and there with bike maintenance, but I was going nowhere really. I never used to stay in bed all day. I'd get up about ten or eleven o'clock but after that I was working with bikes right through to about six or seven. I just picked up the knack from watching people. I've always been interested in British bikes. I'm not fabulous but I can do the job. I've rebuilt two bikes – a BSA and a C15S.

After a year I felt pretty peeved because there was still no jobs around. I used to go in every day and they'd say, 'There's nothing.' There's part-time work here, there and everywhere in the summer – Newquay and places – but there's nothing going full-time. Certain times I thought I was never going to get a job. What really kept me going was pottering around on the bikes. If I wasn't doing *something* I'd go out of my head!

Perhaps schools could teach you some skills, so you could set up your own business. I don't know what sort of skill, but something you could do on your own that you could make a bit of money from.

Geoff Clark, aged 18, Bodmin, Cornwall

I spend three days out of five looking for jobs. On Fridays I come into Maldon to sign on. With the rest of my time I go round my girl friend's, go out for a drink with me Father, play football, play table tennis and I've got me own rig at home.

But I want a job. I want to *do* something full-time. I don't like sitting about, which is why I spend so much time looking for a job. I want to get out and move. If you do a new thing every day, you can only get better; if you don't know nothing about summat you can't

89

get no worse can you? Some people would say, 'I'm not bothering, I'm going to sit at home and watch telly,' but I think that's a stupid attitude. When you go for jobs they always ask, 'Have you had any other interviews?' And if you say, 'Well, I haven't had much time,' they're bound to say, 'You don't do nothing, how come you haven't had much time?' I know several kids with A levels and O levels who are still on the dole, and they're waiting for jobs to come to them; they don't want to face the fact that they've had it. They don't want to go out and fight it, they want to sit back in a corner and wait. But I think you've got to fight for a living. Even if another year passes I'll still keep trying, 'cos one day a job will come along. I ain't going to sit in a corner all my life and expect something to come to me. My parents have been a lot of help. There's been many times when I've really got down in the dumps and I've just walked around in circles and Mum would ask me, 'What's the matter?' and I'd say, 'Fed up,' or 'Bored.' She'd say, 'Here's a pound, pop out and have a pint and a game of darts or something; see if it makes you any better.' And it does, it takes your mind off things.

Matthew Brown, aged 17, Chelmsford, Essex

A lot of kids at school just doss about and think that when they leave school they can sign on a piece of paper and that'll be it — that the government's going to keep them for the rest of their lives. But if I couldn't get a job, I'd move, I'm *not* going to sign on.

Carole Conway, aged 17, St Austell, Cornwall

'Getting a job would change everything'

Whenever I go to the Job Centre the only jobs going are for over twenty-five — 'Would suit retired person.' They think the youth of today are just trouble makers, 'cos we go around with skinhead cuts. If you have a National Front march the photographs in the papers always seem to be of a couple of skinheads — never of older blokes. People are always asking me if I'm going on the British Movement march just 'cos of me haircut.

I went to work in London last year — labouring at Ford's. It was £73 for a fifty-hour week. The job was awful, but I stuck at it, till I came back to Peterborough for Christmas. One of the reasons I came back was because I started hanging around with a bigger group of skinheads. They were really bad. It was in East London and they were into Pakki-bashing. They used to go round with razors slashing Indians' faces. I didn't mind rival gang fights, but when it came to attacking one person walking down the street, I thought 'Bloody hell!'

90

If I saw an Indian walking down the street I used to think, 'God, turn back mate . . . run!' Here though, in our group of skinheads, we've got an Indian and a little coloured kid. It's not racist at all, but people still think we're out to make trouble, because a lot of skinheads *do* cause trouble. I'm sure that's why I find it hard to get a job, but I think employers should accept the youth of today as they are, not how they want 'em to be.

It's boring being on the dole. That's what got me into trouble. Someone would say, 'Let's go out and have a laugh,' and it's something to do — smashing windows and spraying paint. Once I went out fishing with me mates. We'd sat there for a couple of hours without catching anything and someone said, 'I'm going for a walk.' There was this little shop in the middle of nowhere and we tried to break in. We didn't know it was alarmed and they sent Alsatians after us across the field, until we decided that the best thing was to stop and not move. The dogs sat in front of us and we just stood and shook. We spent five days in the police cells waiting to go to court, because they wanted us to admit to another charge. They weren't pushing us into saying anything but in the end my mate admitted it — he isn't my mate any more.

In court one of us was put away, I got probation and a £290 fine, and me other mates got community work and were fined £71. They took £10 a fortnight out of me dole money. After giving my Mum her share, I only had a couple of quid left and ended up in court again for non-payment. They've put it down a bit now, but I'm really trying to get a job. I'd take anything now — even cleaning toilets. I've been for thirteen interviews since the court case, but they just don't want to know.

I've even tried fixing up my own jobs — like gardening for people round here. I tried to get a few of my mates interested in coming in with me, but I didn't have a clue how to set up a business. I reckon they could teach you that sort of thing in school. They should certainly teach you how to sign on, 'cos that's the worst thing I've ever been through, trying to get money out of the Social Security. You go down there to the new claims section and fill in a form to take to Social Security. They give you another form; you take it back, register at the Job Centre and go back to the dole office. Later that week you get a letter saying, 'I'm sorry Mr Baker, you dole's been suspended, you'll not receive any money for four weeks.' I hadn't paid enough National Insurance! Me Mum was at me throat. Four weeks later I go down there, sort it out, and they say, 'Your money will be through in a couple of weeks.' Six weeks later it arrives, and it's back-dated — but you have to pay it all out to people you've borrowed from!

I'm just trying to stay out of trouble, but it's difficult on the dole. If I'm out at night and something's been done the night before, I can guarantee if I see a policeman I'll be dragged into a corner and spoken to. If I'm out with me girl friend she won't listen to me saying that I haven't done anything. But since I've been with her I haven't got in any more trouble, apart from the time I drank a gallon of home-brewed lager at my mate's house and told his Mum I loved her!

Honestly though, I can't wait to get a job. It would change everything. I'm too old to walk around like a skinhead now. I'm thinking of letting my hair grow. But I reckon I'll be on the dole for another year at least. Things will get better, but not for another couple of years.

Mark Baker, aged 19, Bretton, Peterborough

It's great for the first couple of months. It's fun, but after a while the boring details of life, like the washing, become important. People should all have a chance of somewhere decent to live. There's plenty of houses that people aren't living in that could be done up, using the money that's spent on nuclear weapons. There *is* the money; it's not as if there isn't; it's just being spent on the wrong things.

If there aren't jobs surely there ought to be places for people to go during the day to do things, like woodwork courses, or art courses or changing nappy courses or working with kids, working in hospitals, working with old people? Nobody in their right minds wants to sit round and do nothing.

Jo Chadwick, aged 17, Trowbridge, Wilts

See pp. 139-42 for the response by Frank Field

Chapter 7

The Youth Opportunities Programme

'It is *experience . . . and people treat you with respect'*

I did eight weeks at the Inland Revenue. It *is* experience like they say. You're given jobs to do and have to work out the problems by yourself. It's a challenge really. The people there treat you like an equal, even though they're higher than you in a post. They talk to you about their outside life, whereas teachers would never tell you where they went the night before.

Deb Cannon, aged 18, Lancaster

Some people say they're being used by firms, but with the experience I've had here, I've found none of that. You get some bad jobs, but you expect to have to take the rough with the smooth. Although you can only do a year on a course like this, at least you'll find out what you want to do and what you're good at — and they'll help you look around for a job. I get on well with the people here. It's good to work as a team. It's nice to know you're going to get your pay at the end of the week as well.

We have people coming in to talk to us too — about all the things we missed at school. Like we had a doctor talk about contraception and about girls — 'cos we're all boys here: things like what diseases you can catch. We had a policeman come in who told us our rights. When we had a policeman at school all he talked about was capital punishment and whether we agreed or disagreed with it. We asked if we could have him in again to talk about our rights and they said we couldn't keep having lessons off just to talk to policemen.

Dylan Williams, aged 17, Newquay, Cornwall

I don't think it's a waste of time. Being so large it means you meet a lot of different people, and they don't treat you like school kids.

Trish Doherty, aged 17, Lancaster

93

I think they're a good idea for young people between the age of 16 and 19, because it's giving us the chance to go out and gain some experience, which can increase the chances of obtaining a job at the end of the scheme.

I've only been on a scheme two weeks, but I do find people treat me with some respect; it's not like at school. I wasn't too keen at first, just because it was YOP, but I thought that working for the Council would give me a good opportunity. I know of one girl who did a scheme for nine months, and ended up with a permanent job. I'm doing shorthand and typing at night school to get further qualifications.

Helen Ashworth, aged 19, Sutton Coldfield, West Midlands

I've done plastering, building, plumbing, electrical repairs and so on.

You feel you're treated as an equal. No one bosses you around. It's nice to be *asked* if you want to do something, instead of being *told* to do it. YOP isn't training though. Most of the stuff I've learnt is just general knowledge. The day at college is just a big laugh. Most people do sod all, but no one really worries. The kids got so pissed off with it that they used to go down the café or the park for a chat and a fag.

Caroline Asquith, aged 16, Easton, Bristol

I didnae know what I wanted tae do with my working life, but I knew I didnae want tae stay on at school and I didnae want tae go on tae college. What I wanted was a job that was going tae give me experience in different areas of work. I was told about this job. The whole plan is to go in tae youth clubs taking activities that aren't normal tae the club. We can offer face painting and badge making, for instance; we devised a keep fit and yoga course; we've all been trained in the use of the video; we print a magazine called *Teenage Kicks*.

I had second thoughts at first, but I'd already decided that this was the kind of work I wanted tae do. I'd rather it wasnae a YOP scheme, because when you say tae somebody that you're working, they say, 'What do you do and how much are you earning?' When you say, '£23.50,' they automatically know it's a government scheme. 'Oh, you're a YOP.' I hate that word. They look down on you after that if they're working in a 'proper job'. Everybody thinks you've nae academic qualifications if you're on YOP — which is true tae a certain extent, but still doesnae mean that people should look down on you.

We went along tae a meeting about 'More pay for YOPS' where there were six or seven schemes represented, but the guy running the meeting didnae seem tae know what tae do. He was talking about holding a demonstration in a couple of weeks, but he didnae even know that you had tae have permission from the Regional Council for the route.

We decided tae take on the organisation ourselves and one of the guys from CYP printed a leaflet for us tae distribute tae YOP schemes. For our first meeting only thirty people turned up and most of them were supervisors. It was a pretty haphazard beginning, but we fixed a date for the demonstration and set about publicising it.

We drew up a mailing list of other YOP schemes and decided the best idea was tae see them individually ourselves. The Labour Party Young Socialists had a meeting where they asked one of us tae go along and speak and they gave us their support. We also had support from the Unemployed Workers Association. The papers did a piece as well. People started ringing up saying, 'Can you give me more information?' I worried at first, but towards the end it was really good because people were phoning up saying, 'I'm bringing along thirty' or, 'I'm bringing a bus load' and so on.

Many adults were surprised that two young people organised the demonstration. The attitude was that we were going tae fail, because we were young. I don't know if that was a bad thing or a good thing. It certainly knocked us back a bit but it also made us more determined tae succeed. We had an awful lot of trouble with the police tae convince them it would be a good orderly march. But it *was* a good orderly march — we had twelve stewards. Afterwards Mary and I went tae thank the police inspector who'd been in charge. We said, 'Thank you very much for your co-operation and we hope we haven't troubled you too much.' He said, 'Not at all — well-organised parade — you can have a march along Princes Street any time!'

About one hundred and fifty tae two hundred people turned up even though it poured with rain. It was great tae see that many people — you felt that your work wasn't wasted after all. That was what I was worried about — slaving my guts out for two months and no one turning up. I wouldn't hesitate about organising another one. We had a rally at the end of it all and handed in a petition tae the YOP area manager. When we'd been collecting signatures, some employers had been hesitant tae allow us on their premises, because they assumed the petition was against them — but it wasnae anything tae do with the employers. It simply said, 'We, the undersigned, feel that the present allowance of £23.50 is not enough for a forty-hour week.'

I reported back tae the marchers what the area manager had said tae us and then asked for further help. 'We need new ideas, and we'd like tae ask for volunteers tae form a committee tae take further action that might be necessary.'

We now have a committee of twelve people which makes it much easier tae share the work. The next step is tae encourage people tae join a union. With union backing we'd achieve a lot more. One guy offered tae come tae our next meeting and explain the procedures for joining NUPE or TGWU.

Jacquie Irving, aged 17, Edinburgh

'It's better than being on the dole'

The careers teacher told me about work experience programmes and arranged one for me at the Co-op. It was in a warehouse, packing goods, loading lorries, doing stock rotation. I learnt a bit about filing and typing, although I ain't all that fast. I enjoyed it most when we went out to the Co-op shops and I was loading and unloading. It's a bit rougher than when you're at school; they try all sorts on quiet ones like me.

After that scheme I did six months in another warehouse and came on to a community work project. The best part is the day's training when we go out on trips to places like Bodmin museum.

It's better than being on the dole. My Mum doesn't like anyone at home under her feet and my Dad wants me to be out doing something. Out of £23.50 I give me Mum £10, pay £4 for tickets, which leaves me with £9.50 for the week, and I spend most of that on clothes.

Philip Drew, aged 17, St Austell, Cornwall

I like this scheme because it's different. I can have my hair different colours and can come into work in my grotty jeans. I work harder when I'm happy. Some of the other kids here are quite lazy. We had to put some clothes in plastic bags and they'd say, 'Do it slow and we can make it last all afternoon and go home,' but I like to get jobs out of the way. I don't think they're preparing you for work, but it's better than sitting at home all day.

Jemma Littlefair, aged 17, St Werburgh's, Bristol

I'm now in charge of projecting films at the Arts Centre. Projecting a film is an illusion when you think about it. If you sit down and watch a film in the audience you don't realise what goes on behind the scenes. To know that you're creating an illusion on the screen is great; it's fantastic.

There's a union rule which says the illusion must not be shattered: in other words you must have as few mechanical breakdowns as possible or else the illusion of the cinema is shattered. There is an art in changing from one projector to another. People in the audience think it's all on one projector, on one reel, but you're actually swapping and changing projectors. Seeing other people do it you think I'd love to do that and when you're actually doing it, it's great.

Kevin Davis, aged 18, St George, Bristol

After two years on the dole and not working, the people who were dishing out money were getting very heavy every time I went to sign

on, and I started to feel a little guilty and knew it was time to do something else for a bit, so I came on a YOP.

I'm in a work team that does various jobs for the community that
other people wouldn't like to do in Bodmin and the surrounding area —
painting and decorating mostly, and we've done some rubbish clear-
ance.

It's a change from being on the dole. I've enjoyed it — not all the
while — but some of it. I don't compare it to school because it's my
decision to be here; I volunteered to be here. What I'm doing is
obviously useful. You can see the results, like when I painted a mural
at St Laurence Hospital. It brightened the place up and people were
pleased with what we were doing so that made it worth doing.

There's the social aspect to these schemes as well, just in meeting
so many different people. It would be easy to be quite withdrawn after
two years on the dole, but being on my own doesn't worry me that
much. I'm a loner really. Being alone is a thing I can handle.

Barrie McGovern, aged 21, Bodmin, Cornwall

You learn if you want to learn. On a Granada report they interviewed
some kids on government schemes and two lassies said, 'They made us
pick up stones because we were black.' Well, I pick stones up and I'm
not black. I've learnt a helluva lot. I knew nowt about bricklaying,
plastering, plumbing, piping, guttering before this. I can do it all now to
a certain extent. The money is better than I'd be getting on the dole.
I've got more freedom than I had at school and I've got summat to
come at the end of the week. The atmosphere's different. I was sixteen
when I left school and they still treated me like a kid. 'Do this Brian,
do that Brian.' It's different at work. The supervisor we've got knows
what makes people work. If he tells 'em to do something it seems like
an order so they won't do it. But he'll ask you to do it and it makes
you feel responsible. He'll say, 'Right, I'll put you on this job — it's all
yours. If you want owt just ask me for it, I'll leave you on your own.
It's you that's in charge of it.' He'll also send you for orders. He says,
'look in there, look at the shape of things, get the name of them and
write them down yourself.' I could go to college for day release but it
would be just like going back to school.

At the end of this course I could do another six months if I wanted
to, but I'm hoping to have a full-time job by then. I've been for an
interview at a power station and they said they'd probably have a job
for me when the six months were up, but I don't think they will. You
can't blame it all on the government. Nobody can sort it out; nobody
could make everybody have a job. If they made everybody have a job
all the people at DHSS would be out of work! I had one silly idea to
get everyone jobs but it wouldn't work. There's 3,000,000 people un-

employed and there must be at least 3,000,000 companies in this country. If everyone takes one on then everyone would have a job. At least when I go on to another job now they're not going to ask for me exam results; they're going to ask if I've got experience. That's one good thing about government schemes. It's cheap labour in a way, I suppose, but since I've never had a higher wage, I'm not missing out am I? It's a gain to me, because I'm used to just pocket money.

Brian McMenamin, aged 17, Lancaster

YOP schemes are better than just sitting at home, but I think a lot of employers are taking advantage of it. I reckon the employer should have to match the government's contribution of £23.50, since if they didn't take YOPs they'd have to take somebody full time and pay 'em a proper wage. They say that one benefit of YOP is the day release, and I'm taking advantage of that to do A level sociology – but actually when I've been to interviews most jobs have offered day release!

Leslie Howie, aged 17, Wallsend, Tyne and Wear

The only things round here for school leavers are YOP schemes now. One of my friends, who is eighteen, went on a transport training scheme, and he's now qualified to drive all sorts of vehicles, but he can't find a job. Just because you're on a YOP scheme doesn't mean you'll find a permanent job. I suppose they keep kids off the streets. If I wasn't doing this scheme, I'd be knocking round town looking for something to get up to.

Bruce Jackman, aged 16, St Austell, Cornwall

I came back from Guyana in November and applied for a TOPS course to start in August. It's panel beating which I've done before in Guyana, but if you want to get a job in England as a panel beater you need a piece of paper saying you know something.

Between November and March I was on the dole. When I went to the office they said 'What's your name?' – 'Carl Benjamin' – 'Where were you born?' – 'England, Bristol Royal Infirmary. I've just finished work and I want some money.'

I tried going for jobs at the Job Centre but they all wanted GCEs and careers experience; I used to spend a lot of time at Romeos [a disco] with what was left of my dole money after I'd given £10 for food and rent. I was walking back one night and this guy tells me he's working on the Youth Opportunities Scheme. I never knew what YOP was. I said, 'How much do you get?' and he said, '£23.50.' I said, 'What do you do?' and he said, 'You don't do nothing, just sit down the whole day and they give you £23.50. Better than being on the dole and getting £19.' I said, 'All right,' and I just went to the place that he worked and asked for a job, and they said, 'All right, start Thursday.' So I did. It's all right because it keeps people off the streets. You get £23.50 and it keeps you occupied. You could go there and just play music, but you have to come to work every day otherwise you'd be thrown out. It's a place where you learn metal work, but you're not really learning a skill. You won't get a job with what they teach you.

People could learn there if they really want to learn, but if you just go expecting to be taught you won't be taught anything. Instructors don't come to you; you have to come to them and ask what you want to know. But a lot of kids aren't like that; if they know they can just sit down somewhere and do nothing, then they will.

But I got a lot out of it, 'cos I used to ask a lot of questions and do more work on the lathes and so on. People say it's cheap labour and it's just using people to do dirty work, which is true in a way because it doesn't really help you to find a job. It helped me to get on the TOPS course though and *that* might help me find a job. It'll certainly help me more than YOP did. A year ago 80 per cent or 90 per cent of people on TOPS were finding jobs, but now it's dropped to around 50 per cent. About four weeks before you finish they actually phone up employers and tell them what skills we've got. The employer might say, 'Can your man do this and that?' and they can say, 'Yes.' If they know what the employer wants they can teach you those skills. If the employer wants somebody who can jack up and service a car then they can teach you all of that. But it's hard work. I have to copy out notes in the evenings.

At the end of it though I'll be a qualified panel beater, and even if I can't find a job I could put a notice outside my door saying 'panel beating here'. I might be lucky and a car drives round the corner and crashes into something! To do big jobs I'd need a welding set and oxygen and acetylene, but for smaller jobs I can manage with a piece of wood and a hammer. You don't *need* a lathe or a drilling and grind-machine. If I can't find a job I'll think about starting up with some friends of mine. All we need is a small workshop and some tools.

Carl Benjamin, aged 20, Easton, Bristol

At this place they train you so you've a better chance of finding a job. If you go for a job alongside someone who's been on the dole all the time and you can say you've been on YOP, they'll take you as the more experienced person. I thought life was a waste of time when I was on the dole and at least YOP gives me something to get up for.

Andrew Constance, aged 18, Wadebridge, Cornwall

Young people's comments

'They can be useful but . . .'

They can be useful but the trouble is that some schemes use people to do jobs cheaply — particularly work experience schemes. I've been on one where I was working with people who were on £50 or £60 a week, and I was doing similar work. But the bosses don't give a monkey's about what you are doing because they are being given the money by the government. They aren't paying your wage so they treat you like dirt. That was working for the National Trust, but I've been on others that were all right. Some employers abuse it — but not all.

They ought to train you for something but a lot don't. They just stick you in a job that you do all day and after six months you've got nothing out of it. I was lucky because they found me a short transport training course, driving fork lift trucks; so I'm now qualified to drive trucks. The only trouble is I can't get my licence because of the strike at Swansea!

If you're on a bad scheme though, you are not covered by a union, so you're really up shit street. If you're pushed around you can't go to no one. You can go to someone like the careers service I suppose and tell 'em and they can have a quiet word, but that's all you can do. Perhaps an unemployment union would be a good idea. They could push for more money then. You see next month I could get £21 on the dole. For £2.50 more, I can be on a bummer of a work experience scheme for 37½ hours a week!

Geoff Clark, aged 18, Bodmin, Cornwall

I didnae particularly want tae go on a YOP scheme, but you get fed up on the dole. The wages aren't very much tae make you want tae jump for joy though. I'd get £19.20 on the dole, so the YOP payment isnae that much more since I spend £3 on bus fares. I started it just tae do something, but now we're working tae try and get YOPs unionised. If a strike ever happend in a place that employed YOPs then they'd use the YOPs as scab labour because they don't belong tae any union. We're working tae alter that and it would also affect conditions.

For example, the District Council are using YOPs tae restore a wall at the sea front because it's the cheapest way tae do it. The YOPs have tae go down in a cage, but they're not insured if they fall into the sea. The Council says they should have their own insurance policies, but you'd never get away with that if you had a union shop. Some of them do get exploited because they've no force behind them. We work with the Young Socialists tae try and persuade YOPS tae join NUPE and TGWU for 20p a week.

We've started up an organisation called Youth Opportunities Trade Union Rights Campaign and we go round tae the places where YOPs

100

work — particularly on community schemes — and tell them about it.
Once they affiliate tae a union they can go along tae branch meetings
and begin tae do something about the pay, about the abuse of some
schemes by employers, and about the lack of decent training.

Maureen McLaughlin, aged 18, Edinburgh

I finished school on Friday morning, went into town that afternoon
and found out that I had to go to the careers office the following
Thursday. When I went back one of the secretaries pointed to a board
with YOP schemes on it and asked me to choose any I liked. I went
for an interview for one of them, and got the job, but only stayed three
weeks before I was sacked for throwing a hammer at another bloke.
I was working on a roof with another guy and he chucked a hammer
down to me. I realised afterwards it was so as I would hammer something down, but I'd never asked for it and thought he was throwing
it on purpose, so I chucked it back and my aim was better than his.

Andrew Pearce, aged 16, St Austell, Cornwall

'Sometimes I think it's just like school'

Two weeks after leaving school I was offered a job at Lipton's super-
market. It was a six months scheme. They had me brushing the floor
and washing the sinks — silly little things, so that you weren't learning
anything. I used to come home and cry sometimes because they were
so nasty. The supervisor would say, 'Do that — it's your job,' just
because I was on a government scheme, so I finished there. It was like
being back at school.

Denise Hegyesi, aged 16, Whitley Bay, Northumberland

It's interesting, although I reckon some of the things they do here
should have been done at school. For instance you get plenty of guys
who aren't good at reading and writing. They used to go to school every
day, so why don't they know nothing? Here they let you do things by
yourself, whereas at school they treat you like kids, so that when you
leave you don't know what you're doing. Perhaps when I leave here
I could go out and run a playgroup. I'd like to work as a nurse but I'm
not hard enough for that — or I'd love to have a go with the mentally
handicapped, but I think it would upset me too much.

Lise Palme, aged 17, Bodmin, Cornwall

Sometimes I think it's just like school, because we have tae write letters
tae people and you have tae be here at a certain time and leave at a
certain time. But everyone's so friendly; so free and easy. They don't

101

mind if you don't know something. Sometimes at school teachers would say, 'You don't know that? You *should* know that!'

We're running an information centre for clubs. For the first two weeks I was in play schemes for six- to twelve-year-olds. Then we started on teenage kids' magazines, so I had tae do a lot of graphics for that. We learned how tae set up the video, how tae put it intae the television, how tae use the camera, and then did video work with clubs. I feel that I've got some responsibility here. If the other three want tae do something and I don't want tae do it, then they have tae take that intae consideration. If we have a disagreement about what we're going tae do, then normally we discuss it. A lot of arguments have been about what articles should go in. We discussed it and eventually agreed what the best article was. There weren't any hard feelings or anything. We just take everything intae consideration.

Jayne Harper, aged 16, Edinburgh

I left school at Easter. I never took any exams because we had a contract to paint the Kontiki — one of the biggest hotels in Newquay. But because of the bad start to the season, it fell through and it was too late to go back to school and say, 'Can I take my exams?' They'd already put me down as not taking them. It was annoying — I would have done well in maths, science, and cookery, 'cos they were my three favourite subjects, but it seemed important to take the opportunity of a job. After I'd heard the contract had fallen through I looked around for other jobs and took a government scheme in a fruit and vegetable shop in Newquay. It was OK for a couple of weeks but then they started giving me ridiculous jobs like sorting through a sack of potatoes they knew was rotten and treating me like I was thick. I told the careers officers I wanted to leave, but she advised me to stay on — and in fact the owners said they'd take me on full-time at the end of the scheme. So I stuck it out for twelve weeks, until one day I overheard the boss talking to some other bloke on the phone and offering him a job. He ran through the names of the full-time staff, and mine wasn't on it. So I realised they never had any intention of taking me on at all.

Mike Escott, aged 17, Newquay, Cornwall

I keep being offered gardening schemes, but I want something with mechanics, so I'm not doing anything. I get up, go to the café and come down the club — there's nowt else to do, and there's nowt but government schemes. I'm not going to be pushed into one though. I had enough of that at school.

John Thompson, aged 16, Elswick, Newcastle-upon-Tyne

102

'It's a cover-up for unemployment'

You've got to be careful that YOPs don't take jobs from other people.
If they started cutting grass for the Council for example, it would do all
the people who cut grass out of a job.

Phil Bird, aged 21, Hartcliffe, Bristol

They're being mugged aren't they, kids? You get these people who
they're working alongside getting £80-£90 a week, while there are these
little kids doing the same sort of work, plus probably brewing up and
sweeping up, for much less than they're getting. Most of the schemes
I've been on haven't taught me much. Working at the tyre place I learnt
how to take a tyre off, but no one would regard me as a skilled tyre
fitter! The only one I've enjoyed was re-decorating the Grand Theatre.
You got a sense of achievement knowing what a state it was in before.

Alan Myerscough, aged 20, Lancaster

I don't want to be cheap labour and then have nothing after six
months. Perhaps *if* I was offered one, I'd take it. It's just that it's not
very often now that you get taken on after the six months. I've been to
a few interviews for them, but they seem to want somebody who's got
experience. They don't want to start off from scratch. Some of my
friends who are on YOP schemes know there's no chance of a job, so
they tend to give up on it.

Heather Crompton, aged 18, Great Barr, Birmingham

The only good thing is if you know you're going to get a job at the end
of it. With Friends of the Earth there was no chance of a job, although
it was interesting. When you just have to go back on the dole, it's not
worth it and you feel you're being used. The only reason I'm on this
scheme is because I've been told that there's a chance of something at
the end of it. If I discovered tomorrow that there's no chance at all,
then I'd change my placement.

Kevin Davis, aged 18, St George, Bristol

It is nae a career. If you go tae your careers officer and she sends you on
a YOP scheme you know it's only temporary. I didnae feel I was going
tae get much out of it — I didnae feel I was going tae learn anything
from what I was doing — working in a soup kitchen and serving lunches
tae old people. I enjoyed it, but not for the reasons I should have done.
I didnae enjoy the work itself but I liked the people. The work was
merely a case of handing them their lunch. Two months before I was
due tae leave I went tae the careers office and said, 'I'm leaving this
scheme, I want tae have a careers interview.' They said, 'All right,

103

we'll send you a letter.' They never did so I went back and they said, 'Oh yeah, we forgot, you can have one on Tuesday.' So I went back on Tuesday and they left me waiting for ages and ages. They hoped I'd go away I think, but eventually I had an interview:

'Why are you here Mary?'

'"Cos I'm looking for a job. I'm sure I'm here for the same reasons as everybody else!'

'Oh, I thought you were on one of these schemes.'

'Aye, am I supposed tae be satisfied?'

'I thought you were enjoying it.'

'Aye, but I leave in two months.'

'Oh yes, how would you like tae consider this job as a waitress?'

It was the one job she had in the office and by living in, it meant you worked about 12 hours a day with an hour in between each session for lunches. You'd be a permanent slave and it was only something like £20 a week. But I thought I'd go tae the interview anyway until she phoned up and it had already gone. She said, 'Would you not consider going on another scheme? It's better than being unemployed.' I really wonder if it is. I spent ten months at Canongate and I never learned anything while I was there and I don't feel any better qualified tae go for a job – and I'm no better off financially by the time I've paid my bus fares. It's £19.20 dole money and it's £23.50 training allowance. But it's not really giving you any training. At the end of your scheme you may get a certificate which says, 'Mary worked here from then tae then,' but that's all. It doesnae say Mary has learnt how tae do this or that – or even that Mary was early every day.

I think it should be 'Proper Jobs for YOPs' – real work for £30 a week, which is pretty average for someone who's just left school. It would give you a feeling of security. If you go and *work* somewhere it's permanent (semi anyway). You're there and you're going to be there until *you* decide tae leave or get booted out, whereas on a YOP scheme it's three months, six months, or a year maybe, and that's it.

At the moment they're just time fillers, but I think they *could* be made a lot more profitable tae the people who are on the schemes. You could really learn things about work, and use the college training day as part of an apprenticeship for the real job. It could be done without costing much more. At the moment the college is paid money tae do life and social skills training for YOP trainees. They get a government grant. What actually happens is that you go along, take ten photographs and somebody else develops them for you.

Mary Seath, aged 17, Edinburgh

The only thing I was offered by the careers office was YOP schemes. I was on the dole for two months before I took a scheme. It was in a furniture shop, doing warehouse work — lifting, loading and unloading lorries. I used to love it. At the end of the scheme I was taken on to the permanent staff, but then the business was taken over and they decided they didn't need warehouse staff, because the salesmen could do that work as well. So I was made redundant. I was earning £35 a week.

They say it's training for work but the jobs that you want are all being done by YOP people! They've made people redundant to take on YOP kids instead at £23.50, and it's pathetic wages at nineteen for the work you do. Trouble is you can't strike or you'd just be told 'out'. It seems there's nothing you can do to increase the wages.

Mark Baker, aged 19, Bretton, Peterborough

I left in May and started on a YOP scheme in Kenton straight away. That's all there is round here; nowt permanent. I've been doing gardening, but now I'm helping make an adventure playground for a nursery school. It's shite. I'm going to chuck it in and go on the dole. I had to take the scheme, because I was up in court and if I'd not done it they'd have put me away. I didn't want to do it. I fucking hate gardening. I wouldn't mind painting and decorating.

Sean Cross, aged 16, Elswick, Newcastle-upon-Tyne

We take plays into schools, but we can't take 'dangerous stuff' into schools, so we have to keep it lighthearted, which seems a bit daft since the point of the play was to change people's views. If you never bring dangerous stuff into schools you won't change anything. We've just finished this play called *A Bed of Roses*, about equality for women, but it's the boys who do all the taking down of the set, and the girls who handle the stationery! All the same I think it's a good scheme. It's changed my views on life in a way.

If I was the government I'd do away with YOP schemes and create jobs by *stopping* all this spending on nuclear stuff.

Ray Scanlon, aged 17, Lawrence Weston, Bristol

See pp. 143-9 for the response by Colin Bell.

Part two

Adult responses
a basis for debate

Introduction

It would have been easy to accede to the idea that what we should be doing in this book is simply representing the views of young people, without these being explained or interpreted by academics and experts, who already have sufficient channels of communication for their own perceptions. But, since there are a number of books already which represent just the 'consumer' experience, we thought that this book should try to establish the basis of a dialogue, instead of simply providing a partisan platform.

We felt it should begin the process of bringing the important, but often unheeded, observations and remarks of youngsters into an arena of debate about fundamental issues with just some of those people who might have some influence on practice and policy. That may be more positive and fruitful than taking up barricaded or complacent positions with no one listening or communicating.

Consequently, the following pages contain responses to the young people's remarks and questions by well-known adults, who are specialists in particular educational fields. This is the basis of a valuable and exciting debate, which we hope will continue beyond these pages. It is now thirteen years on from the world of Edward Blishen's *The School that I'd Like* – perhaps the most comparable book of this kind in its presentation of the consumer view. But young school leavers are now entering a different world from that of the late 1960s – a world with deeper pessimisms and anxieties, greater expectations and social pressures. We can no longer afford just to let them voice their opinions without some response. We have to bring them together with people who could hammer out something to make sense for the future.

Responses to chapter 1

Neville Bennett
Professor of Educational Research at
Lancaster University

Q. Reading these experiences of first days at school it is clear that some children were quite surprised to go from an open-play situation at home to the comparative formality of a classroom with desks and timetables, yet others found it boring to discover that school was just about playing with Plasticine. Is there any way in which primary schools can resolve this problem?

A. It depends on what the children have done before starting school. It makes a big difference if they've been to a nursery or a playgroup. If children can read before they go to school and the teacher wants them to start at book one, page one, that probably *is* boring. But primary schools *can* find out these details about individual children by having staggered entry — in September and January for instance. In this way, most teachers can do a fair amount of diagnostic testing, either formally or informally, to decide where to start children. With smaller groups, they can give more individual attention.

Q. In commenting about teachers, few of the young people interviewed here liked strict teachers, but if you look at research like your own *Teaching Styles and Pupil Progress* [Open Books, London, 1976], which compares traditional and progressive approaches, it suggests that pupils achieve more in certain academic subjects with formal teaching. Is there a paradox here?

A. No, I don't think so. One of the central findings of our research was that children operating under a progressive teaching approach had more positive attitudes to school. This finding is supported by other research studies, but not much was made of it — or indeed any other part of the research, except for chapter 5 — by reviewers and critics. It was quite a definite finding though.

A second point to make is that there's a stereotyping, which equates 'formal' with 'cold', or equates 'formal' with 'authoritarian'. We didn't find this to be true. We found that 'formal' classes were highly structured and teacher-centred, but not necessarily 'cold'. For example: one woman – a typical formal teacher in our sample – was clearly in control, with children doing exactly what she said, but she would react to a child with a problem by putting her arm round him. The stereotyped image of a formal teacher being cold and authoritarian didn't hold up at the affective level. Although highly structured and controlling, she showed real warmth and affection. So I don't think there's a paradox. I think our findings in *Teacher Styles* probably confirm what these young people are saying.

Q. If children's attitudes to school are formed at primary level, that factor may be very significant in terms of their later achievement. If a progressive approach improves pupils' attitudes to primary school, does it carry over into secondary school?

A. When our research was published, I was often asked, 'What happens to these kids once they get to secondary school?' I had to say, 'I've no idea.' It wasn't our aim to follow them through – we could have done, if we'd had more money. It would make a very interesting research study. Just give me some money and I'll do it for you! You *could* assume all sorts of things: like that children who have been through a progressive system would find it harder to settle down in a more formal secondary school, or that, with a more positive attitude to school, they'd find it easier. You can put forward quite opposite theories on the basis of existing information, but it really needs checking out. Such research would be complicated by the way in which secondary schools arrange the transfer from primary level. In some areas the junior teacher goes up with the class to the secondary school and stays with them a whole year. In some schools they are randomly shuffled into mixed ability groups till year three, whereas in others they test straight away and group them into streams. How this transfer is organised is sure to affect children's attitudes to school – as these young people are saying.

Q. You mention streaming at secondary level. Some of these young people are quite critical of this process. Do you think it's damaging to stream children at primary school?

A. Only about 10 per cent of primary schools obviously stream, but there's a lot of disguised streaming, because although most *schools* aren't streamed, most *classes* are. It's typical of teachers to put children into groups of five or six based on ability and call these groups by colours, or animal names. I visited one school in Avon, where they were in colour groups, and said to one little lass, 'What group are you in?' 'Yellow' – 'Which is the best group?' – 'Red' – 'Which is the next best group' – 'Green' – You're not conning anybody. Kids know where they are.

This method of streaming is understandable though, because it's one way for primary teachers to work with a class of thirty at an individual level. You can give the bright group some work and know that they're going to get on with it, which will give you time to work with the slower group. It's a realistic approach. This sort of disguised streaming also happens extensively in infant schools, which is interesting given the traditional view of infant schools as being orientated towards 'play'.

Q. Can we look at this perspective of 'play' more deeply? Both of us are supporters of the John Dewey model of 'learning by doing'. Is there a primary school equivalent of this? Is it learning by playing?

A. If you're talking about the situation as it actually is, I don't think it does follow that model, because all the surveys at primary level show that little pupil choice is available. It's very much teacher-directed. If you look for the Dewey notion of learning by doing, which you might call 'structured discovery' there's very little taking place. Teachers are still the focal point of the classroom. They might allow some choice, like selection of afternoon projects, but they're the people in control of the classroom and the curriculum – and often of the grouping arrangements in the classroom as well.

How the situation *ought* to be though, is crucially related to the demands put on the teacher. *Teaching Styles* said nothing about Plowden's theory; it said something about how the theory was being put into practice, like that only 10 to 17 per cent of schools were following the model suggested by Plowden. Although I actually agree with the theory – with the individualisation of learning – I wonder how you do it in practice with existing pupil-teacher ratios? It's unfair to say to teachers that it's possible to individualise with thirty children. It isn't.

There's only one way you can do it, and that's to have more personnel. If I was a Head I'd bring in parents, who are a tremendously under-used resource – largely because of traditional teacher autonomy and their resistance to involvement by outsiders. Some teachers feel threatened by letting in parents. In the middle 1960s and early 1970s, when progressive teaching was all the rage, there was a clear split between the philosophy of the teaching profession and the philosophy of parents. Maybe teachers were standing on their professionalism too much – 'We know what's best for your kids, beat it' – which was a great mistake, because they didn't carry parents with them – and still haven't quite frankly. But parents are a terrific resource, especially with the current unemployment situation.

Q. Moving on to a more general point, some people would say that secondary schools judge pupils by criteria inappropriate to the conditions of the 1980s. Would you say the same of primary schooling?

Is it still regarded as a filter process for secondary school, for example?

A. One problem with primary schools is that they don't know what their role is, because there's no consensus about what children should know or have experienced by the time they're eleven. No one has clearly answered basic questions like, 'What should we be aiming for by the time these children are eleven?' or 'Is it realistic to expect them to be proficient in certain subject areas?' Without consensus, there are bound to be wildly different approaches, which cause all sorts of problems for the first-year secondary teacher, who will have very different levels of competence amongst his intake.

Q. Reflecting on her move to secondary school, Janet remarked that it came as quite a shock to realise that she wasn't as good as she thought she was — going from top in maths in primary school to near the bottom in her secondary class. How can secondary schools avoid putting people down like that?

A. This is difficult. The high ability children in some primary school classes are bound to be at the same level as the low ability children in others. Some people would say that children have to realise where they stand in relation to others. There's no way you can disguise it unless you develop a very different system based on a sort of 'mastery learning' model, where you're not concerned to compare a child to the rest of his class, but rather to compare each child to *himself* and his own progress. On this model you divide the curriculum into chunks and test each chunk, and make sure the child knows that particular chunk before he moves onto the next. My experience with remedial readers is that, if you go right back to the beginning, you find that somewhere along the line they've missed a crucial concept, and if you can locate this concept you can make three years' progress in six months. A 'mastery learning' model where you measure individual retention of skill and knowledge at intervals is going to be more use to a child than testing him in relation to the kid next to him. I don't always see the need to measure people against an outside standard.

Q. Are the standards required at the transition point from primary to secondary obvious to both sides?

A. No, they're not, but secondary schools have a problem with which I sympathise. Coming from six or eight feeder primaries, the children in a class of thirty will have had different experiences of mathematics schemes, language, and of science, so you're placing the secondary teacher in a very difficult position. It's not surprising that their reaction is often to take children right back to square one. Given the fact that we don't have a straight-through system this is a fairly realistic response.

Q. Would you argue for a straight-through system?

A. I'd argue for a 'campus' system, perhaps with different playgrounds because there can be problems mixing older and younger pupils at play times. Ideally you shouldn't segregate by age; it's the wrong basis on which to plan an education system. You should be grouping according to cognitive or developmental age. If you do it by cognitive age, though, you bring in other problems. Does a fourteen-year-old want to be sat with eleven-year-olds?

Q. There's another problem too: that if you group according to cognitive age you'll end up separating friends, which is one of the criticisms expressed by these young people. Is this splitting of friends a common experience?

A. It varies. Some authorities allocate children to secondary schools on the basis of ability banding to provide a similar pool of ability in each comprehensive — and that could well involve splitting friendships. If you operate a system of parental choice that would also be a factor. On the whole, though, primary schools have very small catchment areas, so you would expect all the pupils to go to the same comprehensive. Of course, once in the comprehensive they could be split into different classes, but that may not be such a bad thing. It *can* be constructive, because they get to know more children, while still retaining old friendships at playtime, and after school.

Q. Yes, some of these remarks like Brian's and Keith's confirm that point. A recurring sentiment, though, is that the young people here felt they became less of an individual once in secondary school, and that teachers became less intimate and caring. Is this an inevitable process?

A. It's partly a result of school size, which you can't do much about, but it's also a corollary of school organisation. Primary school pupils are used to just one teacher all day, and suddenly, in secondary school, they find themselves chasing a different teacher every forty minutes. I can't honestly see any educational rationale for asking a kid to change a room and a teacher — as well as the subject — every forty minutes. It's the Pink Floyd sausage machine. It's a result of specialisation, and perhaps secondary schools could learn from the middle school model, where there's a gradual transition from the primary-school structure at ten to the secondary-school structure at fourteen. Surely it's not beyond the wit of man to produce teachers who are able to teach three or four subjects up to the age of thirteen to minimise this flow of human traffic?

Q. If you look at the financial resources allocated to primary schools, they're the least well off. Should they be the best — and if so what would be your evidence in making out such a case?

A. I think they're the least well resourced because they're not domina-
ted by examinations. If you're doing exam courses, like O level
English, you *have* to buy a certain number of set books. You don't
have to do that in primary schools.

But there's actually no *evidence* that links better quality teaching
with increased resources. It's a case that's often made: that if you
decrease resources you're going to decrease the quality of life, but
I don't think there's any hard evidence to support this view — I
suspect that teachers simply become more resourceful themselves.
Of course there has to be a bottom line in resource terms beyond
which life becomes unbearable and teaching impossible, but I
suspect the quality of teaching in itself is not affected by initial de-
creases in resources. That's not to argue that there shouldn't be more
resources; I'm simply saying that we can't automatically assume that
better resources equals better teaching. The crucial thing it seems to
me is the personality and skills of the teacher, and that's something
quite independent of available software.

Responses to chapter 2

David Hargreaves
Reader in Education at Oxford University, who has specialised in issues relating to secondary education

Q. Several people talk here about the need for pupils to be given responsibility within the school. How could schools facilitate this?

A. You can only exercise responsibility if you have control over something, and the present structure of schooling doesn't allow pupils to have such power – or even the choice to say 'no' to something. Teachers are very reluctant to concede this power. The situation that Mandy describes where she's reading *Mr Fox* during a geology lesson because she's bored is a good example. She points out that perhaps he could have responded to her remark, instead of taking it as cheek that had to be squashed. She had no genuine choices and he couldn't allow her to have any because that would threaten his control. This seems to me to be one consequence of subject teaching, where one teacher, determined to teach his subject, confronts a group of cooped-up adolescents. It's extremely artificial; we forget how recent schools are as institutions and that, in many respects, they're unnatural places for teenagers.

Q. But schools would say that they *do* give youngsters choices, because there are option systems, and structures like school councils.

A. Yes, but we all know that the range of options is rather limited. Research shows that the options children select are 'guided', which means in practice that teachers are doing an elaborate kind of streaming, and the 'choice' is really quite superficial. Choosing between art and needlework at the end of the third year is not much of a choice. It seems to me that responsibility comes when people are able to make regular and meaningful choices, make mistakes, and can then re-choose. Saying pupils have a choice in school is like saying people have power because they can elect MPs once every five years. That doesn't give you involvement *or* political responsibility. But it's a close parallel to what happens in school. Pupil responsibility must mean the capacity to do things sometimes that teachers don't approve of. Young people must have daily chances to say, 'I made the wrong decision and I've changed my mind.'

Q. How would that work in the classroom?

A. It means breaking down a lot of barriers. I would look very hard at the *methods* of working. Perhaps pupils need to go *out* of school to gather appropriate information — such as into public libraries. Universities work perfectly well in this way, because the students are motivated. The trouble with schools is they get locked into a vicious circle where teachers can't trust pupils, so they have to keep watch; pupils then become less trustworthy because they resent being watched and controlled. I think schools should try to regard themselves more like universities in this sense. Of course it would present problems — there are always problems until you have trust. But without trust people won't develop responsibility, or the motivation to work together in gathering resources or redefining problems. Barriers between school and community would have to diminish. We should be using the ideas of Paul Goodman about people going into the city and using it and its resources as a means of learning back in the school. That probably means involving people from the community.

Q. A lot of teachers would say they *were* trying to make subjects relevant by taking pupils out or bringing people in to talk — and trying to relate that to the pupil's experience. What's wrong with that?

A. Nothing. That's splendid. But there is another point to make which refers back to responsibility and partnership. Sometimes the youngsters themselves will have things to offer and might say, 'These are what we see as our problems, or the important problems — can you help us solve them?' In many cases the teachers won't know enough about these problems to be able to respond, and often one of the characteristics of professional teachers in this kind of situation is to react defensively as if they alone have a monopoly of knowledge. There are two sides to being a teacher. One is saying, 'Look, we are older, we have a broader experience than you and we're going to try and widen your horizons.' But the other is to recognise that kids also have knowledge and experiences, which can be used and built upon, if the teachers will see themselves as having the skills to seek out relevant resources, rather than as experts with ready-made answers.

Q. That's fine, but wouldn't a lot of people, including parents and children, say that isn't what teachers should be doing at school? There's a given curriculum and their job is to teach it.

A. Parents are going to be more difficult to win over than children because they were taught to have a highly traditional conception of school as a disciplinary institution. I wonder though whether we're nearing a breakthrough, because of the collapse of the idea of exams as an automatic job ticket. Most parents seem to have taken the view that the function of exams is to provide qualifications for jobs and, when that breaks down because of youth unemployment, there will be a lot of qualified young people unemployed for long periods. When parents see this they're going to begin to say, 'What's education *for*? If it isn't to get a job, what *is* it about?'

Q. When you say 'collapse of exams' are you including the proposed sixteen-plus exam which isn't scheduled to become operative till 1986?

A. Yes, it's a gigantic irrelevance for so many young people. For those who are destined to enter higher education, exams will continue to exercise their traditional function. For the rest it's already becoming irrelevant. I meet youngsters now who say, 'There's no point working for CSEs because that won't help me get an apprenticeship.' CSEs used to lead to a job. Teachers have been using public exams as a carrot for a long time to get pupils to work hard in school so they can get a good job. Once that notion has collapsed we can tamper all we like with producing a common exam, but the central motivating element will have gone, and people will have to re-assess their positions.

Q. So you see exams as becoming redundant for all but a small minority?

A. I don't think secondary education in Britain will move in the right direction until we've abolished all public examinations before A level. That's not really a very radical view either; it's shared by a number of chief education officers, leaders of teachers' unions and ordinary teachers. What we should do is make it illegal for anyone to offer jobs on the basis of paper qualifications, unless they can show they're directly related to the skills required for that job. That's what Ronald Dore proposed years ago. When we do that we'll be forced to recognise that what we're offering with exams is not job qualifications, but an assessment of educational achievement. And then we'd be able to discuss what the point of educational achievement is, if it's not giving pupils occupational skills.

Q. But teachers will say exams are a yardstick that most children still want to measure themselves by.

A. We should distinguish between assessment on the one hand and a national system of examinations that effectively streams people at thirteen on the other. I'm sure children want to be assessed and to know how well they're doing, but they also need to learn the skill of self-evaluation, which our present education system doesn't promote. It seems to be right that children want a notion of standards – it's true of football, or mathematics or painting pictures. One wants to know if one is any good. But I don't think you can justify our present exam system on that basis.

The trouble is that CSE and O level examinations are the standard that all young people are tested against: 20 per cent go through to higher education and the rest don't, so you stigmatise large numbers as relative failures, who fall at the exam hurdle. Children are often bored because school is where they get a sense of failure rather than of achievement. Youngsters are very realistic at assessing how good they are. I don't meet many kids who think they're God's gift to mathematics and who need to enter national exams to prove them wrong. They know perfectly well. I suspect kids suss one another out in terms of their relative skills faster than their teachers can.

Q. Coming back to what you said previously about pupils bringing their problems into the classroom, isn't one of the barriers the different cultural and class differences between teachers and young people?

A. I'd agree to a certain extent, but I'd add that there are equally significant differences between people of the same social class. I think it's true that a lot of teachers don't know what it's like to be brought up in a poor, or a one-parent, family for instance, but teachers have resources at their disposal to set such problems in a wider community context. I'm an advocate of community education, which means a lot more to me than just the notion of community schools. It's about people locating their experiences within society. Many of the traditional mechanisms for solving social and personal problems have broken down because we've eroded a lot of cultural conditions and controls, through things like re-housing. People are left with problems to which the community itself doesn't offer natural solutions any more — like the transmission of domestic skills from mother to daughter, for instance, or how to deal with old people. It's generally true to say that adolescents in working-class communities don't know anything about working-class history and, if you ask them what history is about, they'll say, 'Drawing maps of a mediaeval village,' or, 'Doing Gladstone and Disraeli.' There's no sense of their own communities, which have deep historical roots. Often teachers assume that youngsters aren't interested in history because they're not motivated by the set syllabus. But if you start with the youngsters' own lives and problems and locate them historically, they will begin to see their roots. You can only do that by changing the notion that you have to slot a very partial and limited conception of history into thirty minutes on a Tuesday afternoon, with the teacher dictating notes in preparation for O level.

Q. Are you saying it's a methods problem as well as an organisational one?

A. Yes. Most secondary teachers think of themselves as *subject* teachers and the moment they move outside their subject they become rather insecure. It's been made worse by comprehensive reorganisation,

119

because the best of the secondary moderns had teachers taking classes for several subjects. The comprehensive school has produced a
much more rigid system with specialists and departments, and even
'faculties'.

Q. Is that why nearly all these young people say that primary school
was a more enjoyable experience than secondary?

A. A question I constantly put to secondary school teachers is, 'Why is
it that eleven-year-olds arrive full of beans and enthusiasm at secondary school and, three years later, so many are indifferent or hostile?'
What has gone wrong? My answer is simple. First, it's explained by
the narrow educational curriculum, where the majority of subjects
are about training the mind, so that large numbers of children
quickly get a sense of failure. Failure turns most of us off. Second, in
these narrow subject areas if pupils find they do not like the teacher
— the history teacher, for example — then they end up not liking
history. Huge areas of human knowledge have been written off at
the tender age of twelve just because the pupil didn't get along with
the teacher. Teachers want to blame the adolescents themselves, or
outside forces, but I think they're wrong. School organisation is
partly to blame.

Q. Given that we ought to be catering more for the majority, what
changes would you like to see?

A. One of the things that would transform the average classroom is the
presence of adults from the community who wanted to learn. Many
of the discipline problems would disappear, because if other adults
were present it would no longer be a case of thirty adolescents bat-
tling against a single adult — the teacher. The youngsters would see
that the adults wanted to learn, and the teachers wouldn't get away
with some of the crude didactic or authoritarian style as they now
do. It would be a major transformation. Schools need to take an
entrepreneurial view and say, 'We're not just for youngsters; we're
about learning for everyone.' And it makes good sense in a period of
falling rolls.

Q. If the people who control schools see their function as one of selecting and streaming and producing hierarchies, would they actually
want to change in these ways?

A. I agree that some ex-grammar school teachers might talk in those
terms, or teachers who work in rather middle-class, comfortable
schools. I don't hear that sort of response from many teachers in
city schools, where there are real social problems.

Looking at myself, I've probably turned against all the positions I
held when I was a relatively complacent grammar-school teacher
with a very nice group of lads twenty years ago. But I'm not alone in
changing — although it's easier for me, being outside of the school

system. What amazes me is the number of teachers within schools who are changing their views. They're still a minority in most staff-rooms, but there *are* teachers who will respond to new directions. In the schools I know well you could find four or five teachers who would immediately accept the idea of other adults in their class-rooms — you could even find a quarter of the staff willing to do team-teaching. These experiments are going on already. Maybe part of the reason for change is a growing awareness among teachers that, unless they espouse certain changes, they're actually making their own positions worse, increasing the stress of being a teacher. But in some schools things have to get worse before teachers will admit a state of crisis. This could produce a reactionary view: 'Let's get back to discipline; keep the kids in their places and do some real work.' There's a kind of Boysonian rhetoric lying very close to the surface in some schools. But a lot of people are seeing through it now, be-cause it's just not possible to keep young people down in a way that was once thought appropriate.

Q. Are you satisfied with the distribution of financial resources within the educational network? Do you think secondary schools receive their fair share?

A. Of course they don't. The undue proportion of resources that's given to predominantly middle-class people who enter higher education is a national scandal. There has to be something like a voucher scheme, which gives everyone a right to consume a fair share of education, otherwise the middle classes will go on being subsidised by the work-ing class. Universities are very distinguished communities and I don't want to stop what we're doing. We do it pretty well. But the notion that intellectual things of the kind we do here in Oxford are most in need of national subsidy is ridiculous. I'm not saying that everyone should have access to university. If people haven't passed or can't pass A levels there's no point in coming, but if you want to develop other skills, universities aren't the place anyway.

I'm not against excellence. What I'm for is a greater diversity of institutions to cater for different kinds of excellence. I object to the notion that excellence is a thing that only universities achieve, just as I'm against the notion that human intelligence is entirely about the cognitive domain. I think intelligence is also about social, aesthetic, artistic and physical skills which are distributed in complicated ways among the population and don't necessarily correlate with scores on an IQ test. I've seen the notion of intelligence narrowed in a way that's highly destructive, because it makes people think they're fail-ures if they're no good at academic work. What we should do now is diversify our notions of excellence and intelligence. Then we must create prestigious institutions in which such excellence can be fos-tered. And then we must ensure that all people have real opportunities to develop their diverse talents. In such a world the response of many young people to their secondary schools might be very different than it is now.

Responses to chapter 3

John Mann
Secretary of the Schools Council

Q. Several of these remarks are directly critical of the relevance of school subjects. Do you think the school curriculum is too unconnected with the real life of the majority of people?

A. The evidence of these replies is that the youngsters are very concerned to have a relevant education and, although quite a lot of them thought that they hadn't, they remained remarkably cool and analytical about their experience. Many of them were able to make constructive and interesting suggestions, like the visits to prisons, to improve the quality of their formal education. I thought all that chimed in very well with the feelings many people have had that a watered-down academic curriculum is not really satisfactory for a large proportion of young people.

Q. What do you think can be done about this in terms of curriculum?

A. Very interestingly, I was at a meeting recently, where somewhat similar issues were raised by secondary heads, who were considering the problem of post-sixteen courses. It was evident that a lot of schools are very much alive to these problems now and want to bring in adults other than teachers — which has been a feature of the Schools Council industry project, for instance. They've been concerned to organise experiences outside school — notably work experiences — and my guess is that there's been a lot of movement in schools since the time when many of these young people were themselves at school, two or three years ago. Things seem to be moving in the right direction, and moving quite fast.

Q. One girl, Jo, said, 'Childhood is quite an important part of your life; it's important to leave school with a nice feeling that you've learnt something, not just relief.' It seems that we give a number of people in school a sense of boredom or failure. Why do you think this is? Is it the relevance of the curriculum? Is it exams? Or what?

A. I suspect the answer is partly both those, but it also has something

123

to do with the way secondary education is delivered. Since my daughter transferred to secondary school I've been interested to hear her comments about it. She's a bright and conscientious girl and I've been a little concerned when she's come home and has said that a particular lesson was boring. That's something she never said about primary school, so I've been exercised as to why this might be. I think that one of the explanations is that she has fifteen different teachers, so none of them can know the children very well, which must make it hard to pitch their teaching at an appropriate level.

I think this fragmentation of secondary education contributes to the feeling of disillusion which creeps over a number of youngsters. It may have something to do with adolescence as well, but organisation of the school itself is an important factor — and that goes back to what I was saying about a watered-down curriculum. Obviously it's very difficult to engage youngsters who find the curriculum increasingly irrelevant. There's a splendid comment here about gardening being about digging and planting, not just sitting in a classroom writing, and another about mathematics being business calculations not just triangles. The question of relevance is very important, and I think it's attainable without undermining standards, because it's quite arguable that youngsters will become a good deal more competent in mathematics if they're doing maths which they see as relevant.

Q. The gardening comment raises another issue, which another person, Phil, puts very well when he says, 'Somewhere down the line someone's got to decide who's going to be white-collar and who's not, and teach one theory and the other practical.' Do you agree with that view or should we be trying to break down barriers between theoretical and practical?

A. I think that remark reflects a rather traditional view of the world, and the gap is not as wide as he suggests. I'm more inclined to think that one of the problems is how to enable all youngsters to develop a sense of self-confidence. Part of the task is to develop a range of practical skills as well as the ability to read, write, calculate and deal with Social Security forms.

As an incapable arts graduate I would actually face the world with more confidence if I had a nodding acquaintance with motor mechanics, plumbing and a whole range of other practical skills. All these seem to be entirely compatible with a pursuance of academic interests. For many youngsters, having those experiences and being able to talk about them would provide solid material from which they could develop communication and mathematical skills, so I don't see the conflict in quite the same way as Philip.

Q. Well, he went on to say, 'Most of the lessons went on price: the cheapest way to fill our time.' That's quite a revealing remark, because, as the Scandinavians are finding out now, if you back vocational education it's enormously costly. The traditional theoretical school model is cheaper, because you don't need capital machinery to teach a subject like history. Is there a resource problem?

A. Yes, I think so. It's not made any easier by the current round of cuts. There's a tendency for the expensive and practical subjects to disappear first, if a school is suffering from falling rolls and having to examine its curriculum carefully. I'm not sure it has to be such a problem, though. Certainly I would have thought seventeen- and eighteen-year-old youngsters could produce something of value as part of their course. Just occasionally, in further education, it does happen that catering students service a restaurant, or that hairdressing students do real hairdressing, or that motor mechanic trainees service real cars, but I don't think we've been successful in taking that sort of progress as far as we could in secondary schools. There's undoubtedly scope for youngsters to make socially valuable contributions through commonly taught subjects. We don't need any longer to go on with the heartbreaking experience of training bricklayers to put up walls and knock them down again. In Sheffield I've seen a substantial extension to a college built by building students as part of their course work.

Q. Connecting this to careers guidance, there was a view expressed by many of the young people that advice ought to be given earlier than the third year, because you have to choose options at the beginning of the fourth year and, if you've no experience, how do you know what to choose? What's your view on early specialisation?

A. I was struck by that comment as well. I think there's been a move in the Schools Council thinking towards the view that it's important for educational and social reasons to try to ensure that there is a broadly common curriculum up to sixteen. That would obviously have to be modified to allow appropriate provision for the most gifted and the most handicapped, but I would guess that there's likely to be a move in the next few years towards the kind of pattern which is much more common outside this country of a common curriculum up to sixteen. It does raise problems as to what extent such a curriculum should include careers education or any kind of pre-vocational experience which has to be more specialised. It needs to relate to the local economy, just as science, technology, history and geography need to link to local culture to be relevant. You need a common framework, within which there could be specialist local variations.

Q. Do you think then that teaching should continue to be subject-based?

A. There are many powerful arguments against this, but we've developed

125

a method of classifying knowledge in western society which is reflected in encyclopedias and the Dewey decimal classification in libraries, for example, and subjects in schools correspond to that view. It would be difficult to try and break away from the kind of mental map of knowledge that most adults have, and it might actually be unhelpful to a lot of youngsters to dispense with it altogether. So I think there's a need for a compromise between the mental maps that we have, and the kinds of skills and competences that we need to develop.

Q. Do you think that the changing ideas about what ought to be taught in schools are actually keeping pace with new demands?

A. It's difficult to do that because perceptions of the world change so fast. It's only within the last three or four years that we've begun to suffer extensively from unemployment. It's only now that we're beginning to feel the impact of micro-technology. Trying to alert schools to the nature of these changes and suggesting how they might respond to them is something that can't be achieved instantly. Many headteachers are very concerned about this and are trying hard to organise an appropriate response within the curriculum, but they have to be very well informed and sensitive to be able to grasp exactly what the issues are.

The sort of creative reaction that's needed to what happened in Toxteth, Moss Side and Brixton is almost impossible for most people to understand, if they don't live in an area of high unemployment and social problems.

Q. One boy in discussing 'preparation for life' criticises school for teaching pupils to be 'bright' rather than 'intelligent'. Do you think our view of intelligence is inaccurate, and that perhaps a number of people fail because we judge them by inappropriate criteria?

A. Yes, I don't think we have a very broad view of what intelligence is. I remember what used to be said in the days of the eleven plus — that intelligence tests only tested the ability to do intelligence tests, and in schools it is verbal and number dexterity which is rewarded. There's also a slightly worrying tendency, which extends beyond school, to mark people down rather than to look for strengths and to build on them. If we could find things to encourage and be warm about instead, that might unleash a lot of energy and commitment that probably doesn't operate at the moment.

Q. There's a pointed remark from Matthew, who'd been unemployed a year: 'If you're going to sit home and watch *Jackanory* all day why have O levels?' If there's going to be an increase in the sense of irrelevance of exams, won't this influence the reception of the new sixteen-plus exam?

A. I don't think we've grappled successfully with two problems concerning the sixteen-plus exam. The first is that it's designed for the ablest 60 per cent in each subject and not all of those will pass. In each subject probably only 50 per cent of an age group will actually obtain a certificate, which means that, taking the population as a whole, not more than 25 to 30 per cent will get a certificate in a range of subjects that represents what they've studied at school. An examination of that kind doesn't provide a reward for a majority of the population, which makes it a down-putting process rather than a developing one.

The second problem is that we don't really expect many youngsters of sixteen to eighteen to find employment. Increasingly they will be engaged upon some kind of work experience, training or education, just as in many other countries − Scandinavia, Japan, Germany and America, for instance. In these circumstances it's less clear to me what the function of an exam at sixteen is. It's already ceased to be an entry ticket for higher education because this is normally provided by A levels. Examinations at sixteen, as we know them, are perhaps not necessary to the extent that they were in the past. Instead we may need to substitute much more professional skill in observing and assessing children's progress. I think that the development of a record of achievement that's concerned with a whole range of a youngster's studies and with their outside interests and capabilities, will become increasingly important.

Q. There's a growing feeling in many quarters that we ought to move away from the university domination of the school curriculum. But, if you shift that academic domination, do you have any fears that it may be replaced by the exclusive interests of industry and commerce?

A. There's certainly a danger of that happening and people rightly point out that the short-term needs of industry and commerce − where these can be predicted − are almost certainly different from their long-term needs, or the long-term needs of society, or the individual. It would be very sad to end up training a whole generation for the kinds of skills that manufacturing industry needed a few years ago! Instead we have to try and think out capabilities that are likely to be useful in almost any kind of society that you can envisage. These are more likely to be skills, competences and capabilities, than parcels of knowledge.

Q. What significant curriculum changes do you think will happen in secondary schools in the next decade?

A. What I'd like to see are moves in the directions we've been discussing. I think this will happen. We're dealing with a system of five thousand secondary schools all over the country, with a profession that is still rather young − the majority of teachers are under fifty. We're dealing with a population of teachers who will be growing older and wiser, but may be growing more cynical and depressed. External circumstances will affect that greatly. The system is so big and so dispersed that it is, fundamentally, a slowly responding system. My guess is that the rhythms will be long and slow and that secondary schools probably won't be unrecognisably different at the end of the decade.

Q. So you wouldn't agree with the prophets of doom who forecast increasing school disaffection and a general rebellion by young people who don't see any point in being in school?

A. I was amused the other day to hear someone refer to the national motto as 'Who the hell are you to tell me what to do anyway?' I think that spirit is affecting youngsters of school age, and that's one of the stresses that teachers are faced with at the moment. It takes us back to the kinds of skills they need in personal relations; you can no longer assume that the pupil population is an inert mass. But most youngsters – as this sample shows – are quite philosophical really. On one of the occasions when my daughter came home complaining about a lesson being boring, her nine-year-old brother replied, 'Don't worry, you can expect school to be boring sometimes!' There seemed to be a degree of resignation in that which was partly to be admired, because it indicated a readiness to accept the world as it comes; it was also, I thought, very disturbing on another level, and the young people in this book are reflecting very much the same sort of feeling.

Responses to chapter 4

John Eggleston
Professor of Education in charge of teacher training at
Keele University

Q. A common remark here is that teachers should do more to treat
children as individuals, and be prepared to listen more. Do you think
that's possible within the constraints of the existing school system
and, if so, how would you maximise such a process?

A. I think it is happening already and these young people are saying it's
happening. Whether or not it's happening in the right way is another
matter.

Over the last ten years, I think we've become less obsessed with
streaming and with subjects, and teachers have become far more concerned with the individual children they teach in school in a way
that was impossible when we had mass teaching, common subjects
and comparatively impersonal classroom situations. With the development of individual learning programmes teachers are talking with
individual children much more.

Certain subjects in the curriculum facilitate this kind of personal
exchange. It's particularly true of the practical subjects like craft,
design, art and drama, where teachers have a chance to work with
the feelings and desires of children in an informal way. The very
nature of the activity means that you can have subject exploration
and the developing personalised relationship taking place side by
side. In some subjects that's still very difficult. It's interesting that
it's people like the woodwork teacher, the art teacher and the metalwork teacher who tend to come in for high praise in these quota-
tions. That's always been the case. Now what we must do is to find
ways of helping the maths, science or language teacher to work in
similarly personalised ways. I've seen some very good history teaching based upon local history, where the backgrounds of the children,
their community and their families were all brought into the lesson
so that the personal lives and enthusiasms of the children became
part of the curriculum. Maybe the way forward is to break down the

129

formal curriculum into aspects of the personal experience of individual children and forge much closer links with their personal lives.
Of course, at the end of the day not all the children would be really
appreciative, because a teacher is still someone who represents authority. He's often socially removed from the children and he represents academic success. Not all children really want to have this close
relationship with such a person!

Q. But a large number of them say they *do* want to know teachers
much better; that they do want to see behind the professional mask.
Are you saying that isn't desirable?

A. Some teachers, parents and children aren't quite ready for that yet.
I'm not certain whether it's feasible to expect all teachers to have
this capacity to be ordinary human beings and yet still sustain what
they have to do in the classroom, like requiring children to obey col-
lective rules. It can work for some teachers, but I doubt if all teachers
can cope with such an open situation and, even if they did, I'm not
certain that it would work socially. If you want a fuller sort of contact you must either transform the nature of the teaching profession,
with teachers like the Chinese 'barefoot doctors' – really members
of the community – or else you have to change the social system so
disparities between life styles are far less apparent.

But it's not just teachers who have barriers; it's also the youngsters. A piece of research was published recently about adolescent
girl pupils in a secondary school. One of the examples quoted is the
absolute horror of two pupils when they saw a couple of their young
male teachers trying to pick up girls on the kerbside from their car.
Instead of those pupils saying, 'Ah, those teachers are really just like
us,' they were outraged. Instead of being seen as 'normal', the teachers were seen to have 'feet of clay' and lost whatever credibility they
had built up in the school.

Q. Do you think it helps if teachers understand more about the culture
that their pupils come from?

A. Yes. When I first started teaching the one piece of advice I was given
by the Head of the school, was not to live in the catchment area. I
suspect that advice is still implicit in many schools. There's a real
fear amongst teachers that they lose professional credibility if pupils
know too much about their private lives. But I think it's vital for
teachers to know about the district, about the leisure facilities,
about local jobs, about family life – about the whole set of conditions that affect the children they teach. Some teachers *can* establish good relationships right across the social scale, spend some of
their leisure in the local pub or the community centre and feel confident they can handle this and still retain their necessary privacy, like
anybody else has to do in a community.

There is another point: about the learning that teachers can gain from children if they're prepared to be open to it. Youngsters have access to many other sources of educational information – through the media, for instance – and they also have the advantage of knowing more about certain aspects of the community than the teacher ever will. If a teacher believes that children can't teach him anything, I think he is missing out on a fundamental area of personal development.

Q. There's a clear expression of feeling here that they do actually want to respect teachers. Often the teachers they criticise are those they feel were trying to 'curry favour'. How do you think teachers should go about earning respect in school?

A. It's very elusive. The easiest way is by performance. If you have a skill or talent that is held in esteem then you've got a good start. I used to work at Loughborough Training College when it had a galaxy of sporting stars there and those students had no problem at all in school! It's also true of craft teachers. Witness the respect with which even the old-style woodwork teacher is held when his dovetail joints fit immaculately. He's done it out there in front of the class with no sleight of hand. One can achieve that in music, art, drama and in science. Anything that can be seen to be a successful performance is a start. On top of that one needs integrity, understanding and the right sort of compassion – a whole series of personal qualities which youngsters are quick to spot. The only trouble is that once teachers have made a mistake it's difficult to put it right. They become typecast very quickly. If children stay for four or five years in the same school, one's mistakes live on. It's all in *Grange Hill*!

Q. Can you teach qualities like integrity on teacher training courses?

A. Perhaps not. Students have to have these personal and intellectual gifts latent within them, but you can certainly help reveal and develop them. For instance, the responses they receive from pupils can provide a quite remarkable stimulus for self-development. We need to help teachers develop their own self-critical capacity.

Q. But once in school, that process of self-criticism goes overboard for new teachers.

A. It doesn't have to. It's important that in their initial training course we make it a central part of their thinking. In teacher training we make two mistakes. First, we emphasise the stocking up of material, which is useful but not essential and, second, we encourage students to evaluate rather traditional aspects of the work like how much children learn, which is fine, but it's not the only important evaluation. We should encourage them to continue their self-appraisal – to keep asking themselves why things have happened and get the message across that almost anything that happens in the classroom is largely a consequence of how they, as teachers, are 'playing' it.

Q. A common criticism here is of teachers who use physical threats as a method of control, without recognising that misbehaviour results more from boredom than anything else. How do you think teachers should resolve such conflict situations?

A. There's no general advice I can give, except to say that if a young person *is* playing up, or fouling up lessons, there's usually some reason for it. It's not often just freeflowing nastiness or destructiveness, and it is worth trying to find out why. But I don't necessarily think that disputes in the classroom should always be avoided. In adult life, some of the best discussions arise from belligerent argument, and often they are the most memorable. If schools eliminate all kinds of aggressive or controlling behaviour, then many pupils are going to be in for a nasty shock when they go into industry, where they'll meet bloody-minded employers, foremen, colleagues, customers and so on. Maybe the school has to give people the chance to work through these situations.

As for Mandy who complained that the lesson was boring and was sent out, I'd say that either there are parts of the story she's missed out or something has been missed out from the teacher training course for that teacher. We tell our students when we think they are boring and equally they tell us when lectures are boring. We may not agree, in which case we can start discussing it with the student. If a teacher really is mortified when she's told she is boring she's in the wrong job. But don't forget children aren't saints either. If they discover that, by telling the teacher she's boring, they can take her apart, they may do so regardless.

Q. What about the resentment that shows through here quite clearly about being treated as 'kids' — especially in the fourth and fifth years, when they felt they should be treated more as adults? Do you think there is any realistic way that teachers can counter this resentment?

A. I think the resentment of children in school has more to do with structural, legal definitions than with what the teacher actually does in a class or how he treats them. They're in school because they've *got* to be there and that imposes a very different relationship compared to Further Education colleges where students have *chosen* to be there. However, although there are legal impediments to a contractual arrangement in schools, what we are seeing now is a movement in that direction. The kind of skills which I now see in the classroom are not all that different from those I used to exercise when I was an adult-education tutor, where I knew that the continuance of my teaching role depended quite clearly on the continuing support of the customers and, if they didn't come, the class would be cancelled. In the upper end of secondary school, the possibilities available to teachers are very sharply conditioned by what children are willing to accept. This often depends on the negotiating skill of the individual teachers in the school. In teacher training we have to help students exercise these contractual relationships, in a way that allows for professional and appropriate work to be done.

Q. To take that point further: the traditional training for teachers is to go straight from school to training college and then back to school again. Is this still appropriate or do you think it helps to have non-teaching experience in industry or business before teacher training?

A. There's no doubt that schools are still desperately short of people who can help children to come to terms with adult roles. A hundred years ago, although children went to school, they were still able to gain experience of adult life in the community. Factories were very much more open places. Farms were labour-intensive and many children lived on them. People worked in open workshops, and, of course, there was still a lot of work taking place in the home. But now if a child lives on a large housing estate, the odds are that the only adults he may ever see working are the postman, the milkman, the refuse collector and the teacher. That's not a very representative sample, and in a few years' time there may not even be those. Schools need to alert children to the way in which adults work, but I'm not convinced that putting potential teachers into working situations is necessarily the best way, because they will only get a very superficial glimpse of other occupations, and because they will know that they are not going to be doing it for ever, their approach will be quite different. Also, many teachers with previous work experience have often come to teaching because they were alienated by the work they were doing and, arguably, these aren't the best people to alert children to what work is all about.

I think we ought instead to find ways in which teachers and children can explore the work situation together; so that they both go into a factory and share the experience of working on a similar job and subsequently use it back in the school. Youth unemployment has affected the motivational devices that teachers can use. They can no longer rely on the carrot of qualifications which used to virtually guarantee access to work. What is taught in schools is going to have to be its own motivation. The danger would be for teachers to see their jobs just as vocational preparation, so that in making schools more 'relevant' they help children become more employable. In a world of limited occupational opportunity this doesn't really help. You have to do something about society's employment capacity as a whole, as well as changing curricula and attitudes in school.

Responses to chapter 5

Andrew Bird
Senior Careers Officer in Avon until September 1981

Q. One criticism expressed by these young people is of the way teachers prepared them for leaving school. They claim that nobody gave them the information they really needed.

A. I'm sure that's true in some cases, but equally I know of situations where any amount of information has been given, and it's gone straight in one ear and out the other. I've had cases where I've asked youngsters to come to the careers office at a certain time, and they'd swear blind I hadn't told them. I can remember telling one person at two separate interviews what to do when he left school; he'd had another group talk from one of my careers officers and a careers teacher; he'd had a handout and a booklet, and he'd still got it wrong and was adamant that no one had told him! Maybe in some cases they aren't told, but it's not so much the giving of information itself as the way it's put across and the way it is received.

   The main problem is this huge divide between the school gates and the world outside: so that what goes on at school is often seen as irrelevant. For instance, if my five-year-old comes home and I ask him, 'What did you do at school today?' he'll reply, 'Oh, lunch was very good; I had baked beans and chips.' Already he doesn't regard home as being particularly connected to school. If that attitude can start at age five, then imagine what it can be like for some young people by the time they're sixteen.

Q. So, in the light of this, what do you see as the role of the careers officer? Is it purely an advisory service?

A. No, that's only one part of our work. The advisory service is simply the more obvious aspect of the job, where we go into schools, we try and help the teachers and we provide a resource about careers, education, unemployment and what happens after school for everyone. We're supposed to provide a bridge. This means interviewing young people. It may mean giving talks; it depends on the school and what can be arranged. In some schools we operate from the third year, seeing young people and becoming known. In other schools it's impossible to do much before the end of the fifth year.

What we are doing in every school is seeing young people, trying to build up records, trying to identify people who need help and trying to build up a relationship with them. We are trying to convince them that there is someone who's going to help when they leave and who will act as a bridge between school and what happens afterwards — and we try and keep the schools up to date with what's happening. Our biggest problem is that we'd like to concentrate our work on people who need it but we can't identify them till we've seen everyone; so a lot of our work is simply interviewing people to find out if they do need help.

Q. One boy, Tony, says, 'Careers spend months talking about what jobs you can do and what happens if you're injured at work — but you've got to find a job first.' Don't you feel careers officers are becoming redundant, given the fact that there are very few jobs for school leavers?

A. No; that's taking a very simplistic view of the role of a careers officer. In an ideal situation I would say that we're trying to provide an overall service. If somebody comes into my office whom I've seen at school, I will have used my time there to try and identify what that person is going to need, I can look at the situation they're in at that stage. What have they done up to this point? What qualifications have they got (because those are important whether we like it or not)? What are their aims now? Having talked to them at school, have they changed ideas? And on that basis we can look at what's available to fit in with these ideas.

So I might say, 'There is a course at the Technical College for three days a week. It gives you a foundation course in engineering. I can't offer you a job since there are no jobs around, but this will give a basic grounding in engineering, which will build on the metalwork you've done at school. You can still claim your Social Security while you're doing it.' But I explain all the pitfalls, what to say to Social Security so they don't cut off the allowances, and I make sure he or she comes in once a fortnight to qualify for benefit, and knows exactly what to say and do. At the end of the course there still isn't a job so I have to provide something else, which is where the Youth Opportunities Programme comes in. I can arrange a six months scheme, and guarantee a day-release course to do the next step of the City and Guilds Course, which means gaining further education as well as work experience. At the end of six months there still isn't a job, so I can arrange another six months scheme and the same FE continues. Maybe at the end of all that I *still* can't offer a job because

135

there's no job available, but at least I've arranged two years of post-school training and education. With some luck it will result in having some bits of paper that people recognise as being important. Maybe they'll continue to be unemployed or maybe not, but I can't do anything more than help plan these two years after leaving school as coherently as possible, so that it produces a more capable individual. Perhaps later on there will be a place at the skills centre for a TOPS training course and, for somebody who wouldn't normally be capable of doing an apprenticeship, the result will be three years training.

Another example might be someone who wants to work with children or old people, or in the community. I'm not being sexist – but girls *do* tend towards that work. Five years ago when somebody left a girls' school and wanted to work with children, there wasn't a thing for them to do at sixteen. Mother's-help jobs straight from school weren't really appropriate for most young people, since they weren't considered capable of coping with that sort of situation. For nursery nurses' college you need to be of O level standard. For residential child care courses they prefer people to be seventeen with a couple of O levels. Family care and community courses at technical colleges are normally two years, which is too long for most school leavers to contemplate. But now we can actually plan something for them. I could suggest they do a year's City and Guilds Foundation Course at technical college, and after that I may be able to put them into the Community Placement Unit of YOP, with appropriate day release for another year. Once they're over eighteen it becomes possible to work in an old people's home or a hospital – and they've got two years' experience behind them. I've seen young people who've actually followed this advice and are now working for the Community Placement Unit, with a full-time job assured them at the end.

Q. So is your role becoming much more of an educational one?

A. Yes, in one respect it is, but I think it's much more than that, because you need to know so much about what's going on in the local area. You need to be in a position to influence decision taking, and make an effort to create things yourself. For instance, we need to have time to go around to small employers and say, 'Look, you've never taken on a young person; it's not that difficult; I'll tell you how to do it.'

Q. What do you do for young people like Lise who say, 'I don't know what to do?'

A. It's usually, 'I don't *mind* what I do,' and then I have to start narrowing it down to an area of work that's within their experience and which they would be prepared to do. Their experience isn't very great so it's difficult for them to have a realistic concept, but usually you can draw out some sort of idea.

When I first came to the careers service the choice, for an average working-class school leaver, was often just between factory work and building. Now with the Youth Opportunities Scheme they have a *chance* to find out what it is they actually do want to do. The money may be bad, but it's better than the dole, so there's some incentive. It also offers one day a week education that *might* be vocationally relevant. Instead of dumping them in a dead-end job I can offer them a situation where they *might* learn something about themselves, as well as about the job itself.

Q. Do you agree with the young people in this book who say that YOP is just a way of using cheap labour to do jobs that would normally be better paid?

A. Although some say that, I don't think it's the majority view, because the number of bad schemes isn't large. The Youth Opportunities Programme has generated an interest about training in areas where training has often not been done before, like catering. If youngsters on the dole say to me that £23.50 isn't enough and they tell me there's no point in doing a scheme because there isn't a job at the end of it, I can only agree with them if they really do feel that strongly about it. But I can point out that it's £7 or £8 more than they're receiving at the moment, and that with certain firms they can have a day release at college, so they're actually being paid for four days a week.

I think you'd find that most young people who feel it's a 'rip off' have other reasons why they're saying it. It's not just the £23.50. It may be that they've heard of somebody who's had a bad experience, or maybe their parents at home are saying, 'Oh no, you're not going on that — find a proper job!' For most young people who leave school, £16 or £17 a week is a lot, and £23.50 is even more. It's when they've been on a scheme for six months, finish it, and are offered another scheme that some say, 'No, not for that money.' I don't blame them.

What I find so hard is the attitude of politicians in particular who don't realise that most of the people we're dealing with aren't happy to do something for nothing. The only thing that most people do for nothing is go to school, which is probably why a lot of kids don't like school. Everybody else is paid: for being unemployed, for going to work, for going on YOP — or they receive family allowance for a child. Youngsters would probably respond very well if they were paid a weekly wage for going to school. It's a normal cultural expectation in this society to be paid for doing things. Perhaps, once a child is over fourteen, the family allowance could be paid to him or her on condition of going to school, and they lose it if they don't go to school. Roughly £5 a week is going to the family already, so why not pay it as a £1 a day for attendance at school?

Q. Quite a number of the young people here had expectations of going straight on the dole, because they knew they'd never find a job and knew that the careers guidance they were being offered was irrelevant. A number were sufficiently disillusioned and pessimistic to feel like giving up after leaving school – or even before that.

A. Even on the most pessimistic forecasts, though, we must remember that it's a minority who are unemployed. At the moment it's 3 million out of a potential working population of over 23 million. Most school leavers will find a job in the long run, because this is still a very rich country with a lot of employment. Of course unemployment is very serious, and it's far worse than places like Japan or West Germany, but in many of the developing countries, or Portugal or Greece, only a third of the population is gainfully employed and, of the rest, half are doing subsistence agriculture, which is almost worse than being unemployed.

We're so worried about unemployment we tend to overlook that most people are going to be employed and need training for this. At the moment schools train children to obtain qualifications, but we don't actually prepare them to go into a working situation and make the most of it. There are very few people who treat their job as anything more than the job description, with set hours and weekly wages. Organisations that do well are those whose employees are active and thinking about their job – why they're doing it and what happens in it. Of course we must prepare people to be unemployed, but equally we must prepare the majority to be actively employed: to play a part in their place of work – to be interested.

One of the major aims of an organisation like the careers service must be to encourage young people to help themselves. Careers guidance is not about telling people *what* to do, but about showing them *how* to organise and do things themselves.

Responses to chapter 6

Frank Field
MP for Birkenhead and formerly Director of the
Child Poverty Action Group

A. A number of things struck me on reading these comments. First,
it was obvious that the vast majority of young people want to work.
Second, all of them put over the message that the first couple of
weeks on the dole can be fun, and then the boredom starts to gnaw.
Third, their sense of failure came across. Although everybody knows
the external reasons for the present level of unemployment, people
still seem to blame themselves. Recently, on my way home one
evening from a meeting in Manchester, a youth came up to me:
'You're my MP, aren't you?' he asked. 'I am, if you live in Birkenhead,' I replied, and he told me how he'd been unemployed for some
time but had managed to get a grant to go to college. When I asked
him how grim it had been to be unemployed he said, 'There were
times when I cried, but it was all right as nobody saw me.' That
statement sums up many of the comments of these young people.
Being on the dole is very much a private grief, unless people go out
and start vandalising, and then the public side of it becomes apparent.

Q. But people still refer to the unemployed as scroungers, and some of
these young people mention a feeling of guilt. What do you think
can be done to alter that perspective to make it less of a stigma?

A. A number of things could be done. Politicians ought to spell out that
people who are unemployed have been whipped into the dole queues
and recruited as the army that's going to fight inflation for the rest
of us. There'd be no unemployment if some politicians weren't so
over-concerned about rising prices, and convinced that the way to
control it is to have a large pool of unemployed. They put the argument more sophisticatedly, but that's the essence of it, and, once
you understand that some people are bearing the nation's unemployment on our behalf, then you have to give them a better deal. At the
same time you'd back that up with attempts to create jobs. There is
an enormous opportunity for one-off jobs to be done in the com-

munity and time for us to organise our training for sixteen- to nine-teen-year-olds on a par with the rest of Europe.

Q. In what ways particularly?

A. The number of West Germans who are undergoing apprenticeships is five times the number in this country. If Britain is to have an indus-trial future it has to have intelligent management and government policies, and a highly skilled labour force to make quality products.

Q. But, to go back to your previous point, all the jobs that could be usefully created in the servicing sector aren't wealth-producing in an industrial sense.

A. No, nor is the dole queue wealth-producing. If we're going to sacri-fice people's lives on the altar books of the national accounts, we have to get the accounts straight. The biggest increase in productiv-ity by deploying machines since the war has been in the kitchen and the home. These increases in wealth and living standards should be reflected in the national accounts but they aren't there at all. We shouldn't think that industrial production is the only proper measure of wealth.

When one is talking about creating jobs it is, in the first instance, about straightforward ideas for putting people back to work with decent pay, who would then be spending their pay packets. If you look at my own constituency there is a huge need for a thriving building industry both on repairs and building on derelict land, as well as a whole insulation programme.

Q. Coming back to attitudes, do you think that Social Security treat young people in a fair way, or is there a predominant view that they're not entitled to this sort of benefit?

A. I'm not sure. I think the pressure in offices now is so great that I'd be surprised if young people are singled out for particularly harsh treatment over other groups.

Q. When there *were* jobs to be had, wasn't it the young and the unskil-led and women who were most exploited? How would you change that even if there was full employment?

A. I think many exploitative and dead-end jobs have been cut by the recession, and in one way we should not want to defend the re-emergence of these. It's an awful choice: to realise that's what full employment might mean. Now it seems they've got the dole rather than dead-end jobs. It comes back to how you can lift up the econ-omy to provide *different* job opportunities. I don't think you will get that until politicians value human beings more than, say, the public sector borrowing requirement.

Q. What do you say to the new penalty clause which stipulates that either people go on a YOP scheme, or they don't draw Social Secur-ity? Do you think it's a fair choice?

A. No, it's not, but I can see why governments behave in that way. It takes an enormous leap in imagination for the government to have machinery where all needs and tastes are catered for. I've taught people who respond to straightforward discipline, and the problem in the classroom has always been having two groups: one that actually feels secure in such a framework, and the other, who can't bear the certainty which the other half of the room craves for. I would have thought that the vast majority of people aren't going to kick against the provision of worthwhile courses. Of course there *will* be people who won't be happy with that, and my guess is, sadly, that you have to go through the process of showing that these people won't turn up and are being denied benefit, before politicians start thinking that there has to be flexibility in the model.

Q. If you were teaching now, what sort of advice would you give to young people who know they are likely to be on the dole?

A. Some teachers in Birkenhead say that one of the consequences of the massive unemployment in our area is that young people are saying, 'What's the point in doing exams? My sister or brother has O or A levels and they're at home unemployed; it makes no difference in this area whether you get them or not.' But that isn't a completely accurate view, because although it is true that the solution for the majority of unemployed people is government action which creates jobs, some people still get jobs and some don't, even with the scarcity now. It's something like 3,000 to 4,000 people being placed in work per month. Unemployment's rising because the numbers coming on to the labour market are greater than the number being taken off. But there *is* a turnover and the chance of a job, although I accept it would be difficult to put this argument over in the classroom.

Q. One of the boys offered a simple solution by saying that the government should stop nuclear expenditure and put the money saved into industry.

A. Of course you can change the priorities of government expenditure. But you may be dealing with an industry which is very capital-intensive, so that a massive increase in expenditure will result in very few extra people being employed. You need both high technology investment as well as other forms which give people immediate opportunities. It's not an either/or; it's a question of doing both.

Q. Some people say the financial security available from unemployment and supplementary benefit is enough for people not to want to work. What do you think?

A. I'd put it the reverse way. We've been wrong in not stressing how severe the *disincentives* are for those at the bottom earning extremely low wages. One wants policies that work with the grain of

141

human nature in giving people incentives. In letters I receive and in comments I hear, people say, 'What's the point of working? You get almost as much on Social Security.' Even though the levels of benefit are too low, the wages are also low and people feel that if they are in work they should be paid more than if they are not. The difference should be such as to make a real difference to their standard of living, even if in many people's terms it is only a modest difference.

Q. What would you say to those who thought it was going to be fun on the dole and then it wasn't? The word 'boring' crops up a lot in these young people's comments. What can be done about that?

A. We need to think of a proper training scheme for people of sixteen to nineteen if, as a result of unemployment, there is going to be a large number in further education. My fear is that there's little attempt to build worthwhile three-year courses at present; although there will be places made available in colleges, what worries me is what will actually go on when the students arrive. I know how courses can just be cobbled together without much thought.

Q. What sort of training should it be?

A. I think teaching a range of skills is the best model. Achieving is about all sorts of things that don't have to be reading, writing and arithmetic, though I think they *are* important skills to have in this life. The sort of thing that Robert Morris said struck a chord with me: 'If only I'd known sooner I'd have behaved differently when the opportunity did exist.' We want to give people the chance to realise how important their educational opportunities are and to go back and reclaim them later if they don't realise this the first time round.

What these remarks also taught me is just how poor people are whilst claiming benefit. One of them said if he wanted to go to a concert he had to stay in all week and do nothing to save up so he could go. But the impression to someone seeing him at the concert could well be: 'He's at a concert, it can't be so bad on unemployment benefit.' In one election campaign Robert Kennedy was being cheered by crowds. To this one of his aides said, 'It's going well, isn't it, Bob?' and Bob said, 'It's the 95 per cent who aren't there that I'm worried about.' It's the 95 per cent of the time of unemployed people that we don't see clearly which we ought to take note of.

The other thing that struck me forcefully from the young people's comments was the shame of it all. Despite all our changes, despite the whole way the unemployment figures are presented, people still feel that being unemployed is somehow a reflection on them personally. Maybe some poverty *is* brought on by people's silliness, but most poverty is made by our society and the way we run things.

Responses to chapter 7

Colin Ball
Writer and educationalist and formerly consultant
with MSC. Now a director of the Centre for
Employment Initiatives.

This interview was conducted one week before the government an-
nounced its plans in December 1981 for the New Training Initiative,
about which Colin Ball makes several accurate predictions in what
follows.

Q. There are many different attitudes to the Youth Opportunities Programme expressed here by the young people. You were involved
with the planning for YOP. What did MSC want from it?

A. MSC, as a corporate body, were not very concerned about anything,
apart from being seen to be doing something about unemployment. I
don't think they had a clear idea as to whether they wanted job creation, work experience, or training. A view emerged of a programme
which would improve young people's employment prospects and
which should try to make up for the inadequate preparation they
had received at school. At that time such an objective could hold
water because we had only a 'target group' of 100,000 unemployed
young people compared to the 600,000 we have now.

Q. Was there a fatal flaw built into it then? When it became apparent
that the problem was larger and for a longer term, did the objective
of improving employment prospects seem less feasible?

A. Yes it did. But there was still the feeling that things would get better.
Taking the sting out of the unemployment figures, while improving
employability, still seemed a viable objective. Although I accepted
the validity of this aim, my own view was influenced by that phrase
of Paul Goodman: 'It's hard to grow up without enough man's work
which is unquestionably necessary and useful and can be done keeping one's honour and dignity.' The words 'unquestionably', 'necessary' and 'useful' were central to my belief that it should not be a
phoney 'make work' programme. Work is experience. It is a more
real experience than this mumbo jumbo 'work experience.' From
very early days I realised that the MSC view assumed YOP didn't have

143

to be either necessary or useful; it didn't have to be something that preserved one's honour and dignity. It was just something to keep young people occupied.

Q. That's a pretty crushing criticism. Are you saying the MSC were just interested in keeping down the employment figures?

A. They had to be. Remember the threefold bargaining basis of the programme? The Trade Unions were saying 'OK, we'll support it, so long as it doesn't do our members out of work' – which is a farce when you know that the situation requires we adults to make places for young people, and share the work we have with them. The CBI, representing the employers, said, 'We'll support it so long as it doesn't cost our members anything.' The third bargaining chip was the careers service who said, 'We'll support whatever is done, as long as we have a very important role in controlling it.' These three views had to be juggled into a compromise to erect the programme, which the government paid for to satisfy the employers and which didn't displace work from adults to satisfy the TUC. So we ended up with the make-believe world of 'Youth Opportunities'.

Q. The biggest slice of YOP is now work experience on employers' premises. The criticism, which many youngsters make, is that they are themselves being used as cheap labour. Do you think that's true?

A. The MSC admit themselves that one in three work experience placements displace real jobs, so it *is* used as cheap labour. But we shouldn't forget the credit side of this – that those employers who are ripping off the scheme are, ironically, using young people to do real work! I have a feeling that it's the 'cheap' bit that young people are really objecting to. When you read the comments in this book about them enjoying doing real things at work, it's obviously not the 'labour' part that they're so worried about. It's the cheapness which sticks in everybody's throat.

Q. One group in Edinburgh speak about attempts to unionise themselves. Do you think trying to affiliate to unions is doomed to failure?

A. No. It's long overdue. I tried to arrange for the National Union of Students to do this when I was at the MSC, but without success. The NUS didn't pursue it all that vigorously and certainly MSC put the mockers on it completely. Any thought that we should allow young people to organise themselves is against the paternalist ethos! But some young people, particularly in the north-east, *have* begun to unionise themselves. Which means the trade unions are getting worried and reacting with the line that some of the YOP placements are substituting for jobs that they regard as the preserve of working adults. The TUC's avowed concern for the young unemployed is so much hot air!

Q. The New Training Initiative sounds interesting but do you think it amounts to anything other than yet more work experience on employers' premises?

A. In so far as it affects young people, it means nothing more or less than YOP. The headlines convey the impression of an entirely new programme for young people consisting of four elements: induction, planned work experience, day release to college, adequate support and supervision − but you can find exactly the same things written in the YOP sponsor's handbook of 1977. The only thing that's new is the rumour − as yet unsubstantiated − that they're going to cut the allowances rather than increase them. The basic thinking is to expand the work experience element that already exists, but there's no real commitment to the other elements of the programme. The whole thing is a political expedient which has nothing to do with education or training. MSC may have proposed it to improve 'employability', but the simple reason ministers have bought it is that it takes the sting out of the unemployment figures.

Q. But there are quite a few young people who are now refusing to go on YOP schemes.

A. Yes; that's another aspect that people haven't allowed for until recently. Young people are increasingly disinterested for the reasons given in these interviews. First they know they're being ripped off at the allowance level and, second, they realise it's 'just like school'. It's just a revolving door back to the dole queue.

Q. There seems to be a feeling though that on the programme you do at least stand more chance of finding a job.

A. I increasingly think of YOP as being like the Hans Christian Andersen story of the Emperor's New Clothes. The programme has been endowed with these mythical attributes of attire − the principal one being how Youth Opportunities improves the employability of the young. Figures are regularly trotted out: at the start it was said that 80 per cent of young people got a job after being on a programme. After a few months it was down to 70 per cent, then 60 per cent and now it's below 40 per cent. These figures mean nothing because there's no control group left for comparison, since there's an entitlement to YOP for all school leavers. If we could only cut out an area of the country and have no YOP there at all you'd soon see how many young people get jobs anyway. These percentage figures have been used as a justification for continuing the programme. 'No minister, don't chop YOP, because 75 per cent of young people find a job afterwards.' Could you prove it was because of the programme? Nobody could! Exactly the same figures were used before we had YOP to show that youngsters find jobs naturally. I think even without YOP you could probably show that 40 per cent of young people would still find a job by the Christmas after they leave school.

Q. What do you think schools ought to be learning from the programme?

A. Let's talk about the 67 per cent of youngsters who leave school at sixteen. Until fairly recently, schools indirectly prepared them for work. They didn't prepare well. They gave pieces of paper which employers interpreted as rough indicators of competence. Now, for many of those 67 per cent, the jobs, especially the unskilled ones, are in shorter and shorter supply. We will have a recession for a long time, so these pieces of paper are no good to them any longer. All one can say with certainty about these uncertain job prospects in the future is that young people need to be equipped and grown-up enough to cope with whatever uncertainties are around. Hopefully, other social changes will take place so that work is shared rather than jealously guarded by a majority of the labour force at the expense of the minority.

As far as I can see none of these changes are happening. The reason young people find it difficult when they leave school or Youth Opportunities is that they have been in this paternalist, protected world all the time, and nobody's tried to help them develop their own powers of self-confidence and reliance. I'm not arguing for schools just to prepare people for unemployment; I'm simply saying that schools should now do what they should have been doing since the beginning of the century: helping people grow up enough to take their place in whatever world faces them in the future, rather than keeping them behind walls with insulated irrelevancies — only to be cast out one day with, 'Tough shit! You've just got to get on with it now. Sorry we let you down!' But the self-interests in education are so strong. Academic knowledge is conveyed in school because it's the thing teachers know best, and they'll make sure that's how it stays.

Q. Won't there be a knock-back effect when youngsters in schools begin to realise that what's being offered in their lessons is completely inappropriate and isn't preparing them for whatever world they're going to face? Won't pressure for change come from them?

A. It could do, but it hasn't yet. It's a good illustration of how remarkably successful schools are in the indoctrination and subduing of the young, ready for the docility they will have to demonstrate later. And should the number of people on YOP who vote with their feet increase, then the benefit penalty will begin to operate: if you don't go on the programme, you won't be able to claim Social Security. The whole New Training Initiative is modelled on this much-acclaimed German system. They'll be forced into the programme, effectively raising the school-leaving age yet again. YOP is actually making young people's lives less manageable and less bearable. It's consuming large amounts of money for the wrong purposes.

Q. Given that the real problems aren't being tackled, where would you go from here?

A. The issue is about choices. We are not opening up choices for young people. For a long time I've thought that from thirteen onwards people ought to be able to vary their diet between formal education, leisure, vocational training and work. The choice at present is that you go to school or you don't. If we could begin to trust individual ability to make choices and allow for them to make mistakes, we'd have a much more rational system, to which young people would react positively. There would be no need for compulsion or penalties. We mentioned some examples of this kind of approach in *Fit for Work*, where you might have youngsters of fourteen choosing some hours outside the school to do a job of work or in an apprenticeship situation as part of their set of choices, as well as time in school pursuing academic and vocational training. Parents would have a more influential role, because you'd have young people turning to their elders as well as their peers for advice and suggestion. Motivation would undoubtedly increase. That system should apply at both the pre-sixteen and post-sixteen level. Why not make YOP voucher-based? You could say to young people: 'You have a certain period of entitlement; you can use it how you like − two or three days a week, perhaps, with the rest of the time for a college course, or leisure pursuits'. You could even go so far as to give them the money in a lump sum, instead of the vouchers. If it was me I'd go on a plane to the west coast of America and have a good time.

YOP should be about choices and trust. At the moment we do not trust young people to make the right decisions, so we insist they go on YOP full-time − or else. The reason we can't trust them is that we've spent eleven years of schooling not developing their sense of responsibility. It's a vicious circle: we educate them to be untrustworthy and then continue to have no trust in them, because we're fairly certain they can't handle responsibility.

But there is a lot of training which is useful and honest in its intentions. We would have to agree that being able to undergo prework vocational training or re-training once in work, in order to adjust to a change in labour market demands, is a good thing. For instance, if there is no longer a market in writing or lecturing about unemployment, I should be able to go on a course to train myself in micro-processors or bricklaying. Such a view allows people to make a transition from one state of being to another, and that's the kind of throughout-life training system we should have. We ought to be able to enter and re-enter in a much more open way than our pathetic adult education system allows at present, where, if you don't want to do flower arranging or yoghourt making, there isn't much for you.

147

Q. But even if the economy does recover, there aren't going to be jobs around because of micro-chips replacing people, so what is there left?

A. There's plenty left; that's the silly thing about it. If there are many more people in jobs than there are unemployed, it doesn't take much imagination to realise that we need to talk about work sharing, which would liberate people for more training, education and leisure. If there are 23 million working and three million out of work, you only need to talk about sharing six jobs between seven people.

YOP has neither influenced the educational system nor the thinking about the nature and distribution of work. It's packaged away the problem and left people with the feeling that nothing else needs to be done. But we should be broaching this question of how we share what work we have. It can't be that difficult to solve. The practical obstacle to the idea of two people sharing one job is simply the employer who won't pay two sets of contribution stamps. For a society which has been able to solve a lot of problems that one really shouldn't be beyond us.

Q. One person, Ray, says, 'If I was the government I'd do away with YOP schemes and create jobs by stopping all this spending on nuclear stuff.' What are the changes and priorities you'd recommend.

A. Precisely those! Last week, in spite of all the monetaristic restraint, we managed to secure an *increase* in our defence spending of £450,000,000 – which is more than we spend at present on unemployment. The enemy of our society is the imbalances and divisions between the X millions out of work and the Y millions in work. These are more pernicious enemies than these characters across the water. We ought to come to our sense about this. I would be in favour of reducing defence expenditure as a straight swap for more adequate choices and rewards for young people. In the long run it's the problem of unemployment which is more likely to bring society into disarray than the threat of so many nuclear missiles thousands of miles away.

If you have kids like I have who ask you if they're going to get work when they grow up, you actually have to confront these issues. None of this cosmetic palliative rubbish that we're giving out at the moment comes anywhere near confronting them. We have to understand that we have some obligation to ensure that jobs, material rewards and economic growth are shared more equitably internationally. If we did make it better for *our* young people – the ones who are fortunate enough to live in these islands – there would still be hundreds of millions of young people and adult people who are much worse off elsewhere. I don't find it moral to simply defend our own patch, which is the concern of the club of the rich at the moment.

We ought to think more widely and internationally and *allow* for it to get much worse in this country — not just for technological and economic reasons — but for brotherly reasons. We ought to be able to cope with that.

Some conclusions

One of Barbara Woodhouse's pearls of wisdom on animal handling is that, if you want to approach a wild horse without causing alarm, you must gently blow up the beast's nostrils, because this is how horses communicate when meeting for the first time.

In a way this is a similar process to what has taken place in these pages: it has been an act of communication between people unknown to each other who have exchanged thoughts and feelings across generations. The adult specialists have responded to the young people's observations. Ideas have been voiced and breathed and, despite some disagreements, a striking rapport has emerged, as if people were saying, 'I feel just the same; I know what you mean; we share the same views.'

Some of these shared perspectives point a way forward for the future.

It seems clear from the remarks in this book that we must begin to alter our notion of what it means to be intelligent. 'There's a difference between being intelligent and being bright. Bright is knowing what's going on and looking after yourself; intelligence is just someone knowing books. They don't teach you to be bright at school,' says Tony Hunt in chapter 5. It is plain crazy to treat a majority of our young people each year as if they were failures. Only one third of our school leavers go on to any form of further education after the age of sixteen. Does that mean the rest are stupid? We certainly treat them as if they were by judging them against the academic standards appropriate to the minority, even though we all know that academic achievement is not the only yardstick of success.

It is in this knowledge that groups like Education for Capability have tried recently to correct some of these misconceptions and imbalances. It has urged a view of achievement which is not just about being good at academic things, but is about being capable in a whole range of activities: making and doing, instead of just thinking and reflecting.

150

Embedded in our social fabric and flowing through school to the outside world is a division between those who think and those who do: the theoretical and the practical; the manager and the labourer; the professional executive and the manual worker. It is more complicated than that, of course, with boundary edges blurred, but it is undoubtedly a divided system which does not stop at exam achievement, but goes on to allocate job prospects and privileges on the basis of a narrow view of human ability and how we should reward it.

If we sweep this view aside and begin to credit achievement defined in wider terms, we are faced by the awesome prospect that we will need to look again at the way we distribute rewards and status and all those other things which at the moment spring from the present notion of what it means to be an educated person.

'What do a cow and a sparrow have in common?' asked an eleven-plus exam question. The boy who answered that they each ended in OW was not 'correct' since they are, 'of course', both warm-blooded animals. But the alternative reply of Frank Muir and Denis Norden is worth noting. 'What a cow and a sparrow have in common is that they've both got four legs . . . except the sparrow . . . .' Apart from its sparkling wit, what is noteworthy about that answer is its complete rejection of the question. And that is the way we should dismiss narrow definitions of intelligence, as is underlined by a number of comments in both sections of this book.

In reading everyone's observations in these pages you also couldn't fail to be struck by a feeling of depression, if not desperation, about job prospects from youngsters and adults alike. 'I felt a bit of sympathy for the kids rioting, because I know what it's like myself,' said John Masefield in chapter 6, and this sentiment was echoed by Colin Ball: 'Young people are becoming increasingly disinterested with YOP. First, they know they're being ripped off at the allowance level, and, second, they realise it's just like school. It's a revolving door back to the dole queue.' Of course, we *do* have an unemployment problem, but the real issues are about how we define the problem and how we distribute our resources. If I have a full cup of coffee but no more in the jar, and you also want some, I will share what I already have with you, unless I am selfish and greedy. It is the message we teach young children in urging them to share toys. And yet, when it comes to wealth and work we are not so keen to treat people as if they had equal needs and rights and share things out.

It is perhaps ironic that in the 1950s and 1960s the technological revolution was seen as ushering in a Utopian world in which people would be freed from mundane employment and where education for leisure was the key process to prepare people to lead more richly fulfilling lives. Of course some of the more menial jobs *have* disappeared, but, as Frank Field points out, those school leavers who would have taken these kinds of jobs ten years ago can find no replacement except the make-believe world of YOP or the dole queue. For many of them – as evidenced by the comments here – enforced leisure is not their idea of a fulfilling life. Only one person out of the seventy interviewed was happy to be unemployed. The rest wanted to work: to be in a job and earning money in accordance with the adult status they felt was their right.

There are other ways of looking at this problem of unemployment. Two years ago we met with the Deputy Director General of UNESCO in his Paris office overlooking the École Militaire where the President of France was being escorted, as we watched, into a helicopter to be whisked away to a weekend retreat.

'Look at it all out there,' mused our host, gesturing expansively towards the streets of Paris beyond his window. 'It's all too big, too fast. No one can make sense of the world any more or find any meaning because we organise things so stupidly. We could solve the unemployment problem in one stroke all over Europe until the end of the century if we simply reduced the working week for everyone by five hours.'

Why are we not doing that? What interests are being served by keeping things as they are?

Since that time we have both visited other countries to look at links between work and education in the context of the researches of Ettore Gelpi, Director of the UNESCO Lifelong Education Unit. The Norwegians, known better, with their climate, as 'God's Frozen People', manage to have 85 per cent of their sixteen-year-olds going on to further education. Their upper-secondary schools for the 16–19 age range are dedicated to the breakdown of educational and social barriers between the theoretical and the practical, to the removal of early and narrow specialisms, and to a much more rational system of assessment which builds on individuals' strengths rather than underlying weaknesses. If they can do it, why can't we at least try?

What *is* 'Lifelong Education'? It is what it says: a way of looking at education as a continuous process throughout life, not just something which takes place between the ages of five and sixteen in buildings called 'schools'. It is about making provision for learning at all ages in all parts including places of work: not just learning how to do a job better in a vocational training way, but learning also to organise our work, to understand, and if necessary, to change it. To promote lifelong education is to promote ways of achieving these things. Instead of just being about sitting in classrooms learning algebra, it is about participating in discussions and decisions about the planned new ring road nearby or the way the factory decides its prices. All this is about developing minds and skills. It is about being questioning and critical, about being

152

able to identify issues, to eliminate false arguments, to plan ahead, to link consequences to actions, and to compare and evaluate different evidence.

It is, in a way, to do philosophy because philosophy is not just about questions like 'Is there a God?', 'Is there life after death?' 'What is truth?' Philosophy is about thinking clearly, and analysing and bringing to the practical problems of engineering or selling cars the various tools of analysis. 'What does education do for someone? What does English actually do? What it *should* do is teach you to think and to ask questions,' remarked 'Tory Crimes' in chapter 3. We must get away from thinking about education as being made up of specialised subjects reflected in the school curriculum. To be educated is to be skilled in enquiry, to be skilled at analysing and applying that analysis in action. It is to be prepared to tackle or surmount a problem anywhere we may find it whether at home or at work. In order to prepare people for a world of uncertain work where they may have to change their job three or four times in a life span, we cannot afford to train them just for specialist things. Instead, we have to train people to be good at solving problems, whatever they are about.

Karen Myerscough talks about her father's death on page 29 in chapter 2: 'The school knew what had happened but they didn't talk about it,' she says, and fuels the argument put by David Hargreaves and John Eggleston for teachers to recognise that the pupil's own experiences must also be a starting point for discussions.

We have to teach people how to learn, so that they can apply themselves to any situation in which they might be. You can only learn problem-solving processes by actively working through them, and you will be more motivated to do this if you are engaged with a problem which is relevant or interesting. That must be the way of education in in the future. Marcel Rosari's 'They don't teach you what you really want to learn, like about sex. I had to learn about it on my own: trial and error: hit and miss,' sums up one dilemma rather poignantly. John Mann put it slightly differently: 'As an incapable arts graduate I would actually face the world with more confidence if I had a nodding acquaintance with motor mechanics, plumbing, and a whole range of other practical skills.'

If we look at our problems in western education they are basically those of the world we live in. There is an erosion of family networks and communities. This is made worse by the way we organise our lives and institutions. Why don't we make links between school and community so that young and old share and help each other? 'You don't do anything in school about the mentally or physically handicapped, so you see them as something apart from you,' says Mandy in chapter 3. 'If you could go in as a helper – not taken in so that you just stare at them — but to work with them, help them and talk to them, you'd see them very differently.' Is this problem a result of territory protection? Is the divide between mental and manual simply an attempt to protect class status? Is the economic split within nations, which is reinforced by unemployment, actually about a protection of work and wealth by those who possess it and would keep it for themselves — so that job creation schemes become transit camps for the dispossessed? For them, like all refugees everywhere, it is unclear what future lies ahead or where they could move on to, if we do not change the way we organise things.

Let us not, in all this, be complacent or blind to the wider problems.

One third of our world population remains illiterate.

There are 350 million unemployed in the southern hemisphere of the globe.

There will be 350 million people in the world who will be receiving no formal education at all by the year 1985.

There are over 70 million young people forced by economic circumstances into child labour before the age of twelve.

And yet, with all this around us we complain, and strive forever after the word made flesh in glossy images of consumer society: luxury, wealth and power. It is a material rebirth for which we die in the spirit. Unfortunately the young have inherited the materialism of their parents. It is unrealistic to expect them to discard it without a lead from their elders. It is those of us in work who must take the initiative. *We* have to make cuts in living standards and recognise that the sharing process must begin with ourselves. We can no longer hang on to a disproportionate share of the world's wealth. 'If they could,' said the Navaho Indians, 'the white man would divide the earth into titles of ownership, as if men could possess the wind or the air we breathe.'

But we can possess ourselves and be our own person, through education. In understanding, through the breathing of words, we can learn about things and each other.

Jo said it all in chapter 3: 'If you need people and they need you, you don't talk about the weather, you start to talk about yourself and your feelings, and their feelings and their views on things. . . . Communication is very, very important.'

Appendix 1

Names and locations of interviewees

Ley Alberici	(17)	Great Barr, Birmingham
Helen Ashworth	(18)	Sutton Coldfield, West Midlands
Caroline Asquith	(16)	Easton, Bristol
Tracy Atkinson	(16)	Longbenton, Newcastle-upon-Tyne
Mark Baker	(19)	Bretton, Peterborough
Deborah Barton	(16)	Longbenton, Newcastle-upon-Tyne
Carl Benjamin	(20)	Easton, Bristol
Phil Bird	(21)	Hartcliffe, Bristol
Matthew Brown	(17)	Chelmsford, Essex
Angela Burstow	(17)	Callington, Cornwall
Deb Cannon	(18)	Lancaster
Brian Carr	(17)	Forest Hill, Newcastle-upon-Tyne
Jo Chadwick	(17)	Trowbridge, Wilts
Geoff Clark	(18)	Bodmin, Cornwall
Joanne Clark	(17)	Chelmsford, Essex
Andrew Constance	(18)	Wadebridge, Cornwall
Carole Conway	(17)	St Austell, Cornwall
'Tory Crimes'	(18)	Glasgow
Heather Crompton	(18)	Great Barr, Birmingham
Sean Cross	(16)	Elswick, Newcastle-upon-Tyne
Catherine Crowe	(17)	Wardley, West Midlands
Cheryl Davidson	(17)	Bretton, Peterborough
Kevin Davis	(18)	St George, Bristol
Trish Doherty	(17)	Lancaster
Philip Drew	(17)	St Austell, Cornwall
Mike Escott	(17)	Newquay, Cornwall
Beverley Fenwick	(17)	Whitley Bay, Northumberland
Matthew Fforde	(17)	Easton, Bristol
Janet Gould	(17)	Bonsall, Derbyshire
Yvonne Gray	(19)	Marchmont, Edinburgh
Jayne Harper	(16)	Edinburgh
Denise Hegyesi	(16)	Whitley Bay, Northumberland
Leslie Howie	(17)	Wallsend, Tyne and Wear

Tony Hunt	(17)	Lawrence Weston, Bristol
Jacquie Irving	(17)	Edinburgh
Maxine Irving	(19)	Camelford, Cornwall
Bruce Jackman	(16)	St Austell, Cornwall
Andy James	(20	Lawrence Weston, Bristol
Kristine King	(18)	Bretton, Peterborough
Wayne Lansdown	(19)	Knowle, Bristol
Jemma Littlefair	(17)	St Werburgh's, Bristol
Barrie McGovern	(21)	Bodmin, Cornwall
Maureen McLaughlin	(18)	Edinburgh
Brian McMenamin	(17)	Lancaster
Gordon MacMillan	(23)	Baptist Mills, Bristol
John Masefield	(19)	Kingstanding, Birmingham
Ronny Moore	(17)	Southminster, Essex
Robert Morris	(17)	Sutton Coldfield, West Midlands
Alan Myerscough	(20)	Lancaster
Karen Myerscough	(17)	Lancaster
Audrey Nelson	(18)	Edinburgh
Nicola Northway	(16)	Longbenton, Newcastle-upon-Tyne
Lise Palme	(17)	Bodmin, Cornwall
Kerry Parkes	(21)	Great Barr, Birmingham
Andrew Pearce	(16)	St Austell, Cornwall
David Purves	(16)	Edinburgh
Wanda Raven	(17)	Kingstanding, Birmingham
Chris Rich	(18)	Easton, Bristol
Stephen Rice	(16)	Elswick, Newcastle-upon-Tyne
Marcel Rosari	(18)	St Austell, Cornwall
Colin Ryder	(19)	Bonsall, Derbyshire
Ray Scanlon	(17)	Lawrence Weston, Bristol
Andrew Seal	(19)	Great Barr, Birmingham
Mary Seath	(17)	Edinburgh
Keith Shoulder	(17)	Elswick, Newcastle-upon-Tyne
Mandy Smith	(19)	Withywood, Bristol
John Thompson	(16)	Elswick, Newcastle-upon-Tyne
Dylan Williams	(17)	Newquay, Cornwall
Lynne Wooders	(17)	St Austell, Cornwall
Martin Yates	(18)	Kingstanding, Birmingham

Appendix 2

Questions put to young people interviewed

The following is a list of the questions I drew up before the series of interviews. In no sense were they rigidly adhered to — either in content or sequence — but they formed the basis of the discussion, and a useful check list of topics covered.

After the interviews, I asked each person to fill in a short questionnaire to provide me with factual information — about schools, jobs or YOP schemes, exams and interests, and attitudes to work and unemployment — which supplemented the interview questions.

Primary school

1 Whereabouts was it?
2 Can you describe the school?
3 Did you enjoy it/not enjoy it?
4 What did you enjoy about it?
5 What didn't you like about it?
6 What teachers did you like? Why?
7 Did you have many friends?
8 How do you think you got on?
9 Were your parents interested in what you were doing?
10 Can you remember any particular incidents?

Secondary school

1 Did you look forward to going?
2 What do you remember about the move from primary school — like your first day?
3 How did it compare to primary school?
4 Can you describe the school?
5 What did you enjoy about (a) subjects (b) teachers?
6 What didn't you like about (a) subjects (b) teachers (c) rules?
7 Why did you enjoy or not enjoy these?
8 Did you feel involved with the school in any way?
9 Did you get into any trouble?

10 What were your parents' attitudes to school?
11 Did you feel there were things about school that could be improved or changed?
12 If you were running a school what would you change?
13 How did you get on with teachers?
14 What makes a good teacher do you think?
15 Can you remember situations where you thought teachers were treating kids unfairly? or vice versa?
16 Was there a noticeable sex bias in the teaching or in subject choice?
17 Towards the end did you feel what you were doing was useful?
18 How much help did you get about preparation for leaving school?
19 What other things would you have liked to do?
20 What happened on your last day?
21 How do you think school has helped you in terms of what you're doing now?

Leaving school and starting work

1 What did you want to do whilst you were at school?
2 What help did you get from the careers office?
3 What help did you get from other people like friends, parents, etc.?
4 What did you expect would happen when you left school?
5 What *did* happen? Can you describe leaving school and looking for jobs?

If employed

1 How long did it take you to find a job?
2 What are you doing now? Earning?
3 Is it what you want to do?
4 Has what you did at school helped at all?
5 In what ways?
6 What matters to you about a job? Money?
7 What do you want to be doing in five years?
8 What do you do outside of work?
9 How would you improve your work situation if you were running the place?
10 Do you think schools should be doing anything different to prepare people for work?

If unemployed

What are you doing — YOP scheme or dole?

If YOP scheme

1 What are you doing? Do you like it?
2 What do you enjoy/not enjoy about it?

3   How does it compare to school?
4   Are attitudes of supervisors the same as teachers?
5   Are you learning anything useful?
6   Will it help you towards a job?
7   Do you think YOP schemes are a good idea? What other possi-
     bilities could you suggest?
8   How could you improve it?

If on the dole

1   For how long? How much do you get?
2   Have you spent much time looking for work?
3   Do you like being on the dole?
4   What do you do with your time?
5   Have you many friends on the dole?
6   How do you budget the money?
7   What is your parents' attitude?
8   Do you think school could have done anything to prepare you for
     this?
9   What do you think the government could do to reduce unemploy-
     ment?
10   What will you do if you're still on the dole in a year?
11   Do you think unemployment explains the violence in certain
     cities recently?
12   What would you like to do?

General

1   Looking back on school, are there suggestions you could make to
     improve it or change it, make it more useful for people when they
     leave?
2   What things have influenced your attitudes most? Teachers?
     Parents? Friends?
3   What do you think will happen if unemployment continues at
     such a high level?
4   What would you do if you were running the country?

Appendix 3

Index of interviewees